DEDICATION:

This work is dedicated to my Papa,
John Michener Richardson "BIG JOHN".
I carry you everywhere. Your legacy will forever
live on through me. I miss you dearly

The Ace of Spades (also known the spadille)
is traditionally the highest card in the deck.
The actual value of the card varies
from game to game.
In legend and folklore,
It is known as the death card.

Ace Of Spades

CHAPTER 1

Brrrring, "Ok class you are dismissed, don't forget to read chapters...blah blah blah...." Mrs. Calhoun and the bell ending 6th period broke me out of my trance. "Six periods down one more to go" I thought to myself as I gathered my things and was out the door before anybody could notice. One more month of school and I'll be graduating. I'm not supposed to graduate until next year. However, because my grades are the shit, I'm graduating early and I can't wait. I walked to my cousins' locker and waited on her. I looked down the hall at some boys picking on some nerdy girl, you know throwing her books on the floor. They knew better then to try me like that, there would be hell to pay.

My name is Jazzell Harris, but everyone calls me Jazzy. I'm from the east side of Winston-Salem, NC also known as Tre-4. I'm seventeen years old and the oldest child of my Mama's three. I am 5'4", with the body of a grown woman. Unlike my sisters who, both have beautiful dark chocolate skin, my tone is more like caramel. My sisters and I were blessed with naturally curly hair but I decided to lock my hair when I was thirteen years old, my locs fell just above my plump butt.

My middle sister Cynthia aka Cyn is fifteen, she is the quiet type always has her head in a book. Don't fuck with her though or you will see that dark side come out. Mostly she stayed to herself so few people have ever seen that side of her. My younger sister Nakia aka Kia is 13, she is the typical jock. She is on every sports team in the damn school tennis, basketball, soccer, she even played rugby.

I love my sisters but I'm closer to my two cousins Lil Ray and Tan. Even though the three of us are as different as morning afternoon and night we have a bond that is unbreakable. Lil Ray is the only son of my aunt Tissie and is ruthless just like his Mama. When his dad was sentenced to life in prison a few years ago, Lil Ray became the man of the house. He started working for our Papa as a runner, basically he would take the dope boys their product when they needed to re-up and bringing Big John back his money. Now at the young age of seventeen he is running his own block.

Tan and I've always been like two peas in a pod. Maybe cause our birthdays are a day apart and we are the exact same age. She is the only child of my uncle Troy. Her mom left my uncle and moved to Atlanta and is now remarried. She wanted to take Tan with her but being that Tan was of age at the time of the divorce the courts let her choose which parent she wanted to live with, it is obvious she decided to stay with her dad. She is the creative one of the trio. She can take a $15 outfit from Walmart and once it leaves her sewing machine you would swear it was designer. The three of us are inseparable.

Just to give you a little background, both of my parents were born and raised in Winston Salem and are products of two of the biggest drug dealing families in the Tre. My Mamas' father, John Harris aka Big John is one of the biggest and most respected hustlers in the city. So, it is understood that my uncles and cousins followed suit. My grandfather is like god to me, he is untouchable. Everyone loves him and treats him as if he can walk on water. It always amazes me how he could walk in a crowded room and everyone would break their neck to speak or acknowledge him. I'm always right there by his side, his "educated owl" is what he calls me. One, because I'm smart as a whip, I can solve any math problem in my head without missing a beat and two because I was noisy. He always says "Damn Jazzy, your favorite word is WHO? Like a damn owl"

My dad's father Townsend Louis aka Towns, is also a well-respected hustler in my small hometown. But unlike Big John, Towns is respected out of fear. The hood respects Big John because he shows love and makes sure everyone is good. He used the money he made from selling drugs and opened varies businesses throughout the city and hired people from around my hood. This was his way of giving back to the community. Towns on the other hand ruled his squad by instilling fear in them. I saw him beat a nigga on the block within inches of his life all because he owed him $100.

The two men hate each other because they are rivals, which separated the city. Big Johns crew ran the East and South side while Towns had the North and West side on lock. The two crews would beef whenever they ran into each other or someone was caught trying to slang on the wrong side of town. The hatred grew when my parents decided that they were in love and couldn't live without each other, merging the two families together. However, out of love for my Mama, my Papa decided to reach out to Towns and call a truce. The two men agreed to squash the beef if they stayed clear of each other and neither crew would hustle outside of their boundaries. My sisters and I, never got close to my father side, we were raised by and are closer to my Mama's side of the family.

My Mama, Tori Harris, and my dad, Calvin Louis always had a toxic relationship. It got worst after I was was born. Why my mom had two more kids by him is beyond me. My dad was just like his father, he wanted everyone to fear him, including my Mama. I remember being awaken out of my sleep many nights by my dad and my Mama arguing and my dad breaking shit. I always was afraid of my dad; he was like a damn rattle snake, just mean as hell and my Papa hated him with a passion.

My dad worked for his father so financially we were straight at first. Until my dad broke the first rule of the game: to never get high off your own supply. I watched him go from selling dope, to putting it up his nose to finally smoking crack. His dad eventually cut him off after money and product kept coming up short. Soon after that my Mama divorced him and it was downhill for him. Straight crackhead, stealing and robbing people to get high. He eventually robbed the wrong person and they put a bullet in his head. I was hurt only because I could see how much it hurt my Mama to learn her kids father had been killed. I got over that shit quick, as did my Mama after the check cleared from that hefty insurance policy she had on my dad. After he was killed, she used the insurance money and opened two hair salons, and hired my two aunts and my grandmother all help operate.

We live in the East side of Winston-Salem in City View Projects, right off Old Greensboro Rd. otherwise known as O.G.B. Even though my family have enough money to move out of the hood, my Papa says he feels more comfortable amongst his people. My family is HUGE and my Grandparents raised us to be tight and to look out for each other. My grandparents had seven children, five girls and two boys, so my family consist of mostly women and we were all remarkably beautiful. We got our looks from my grandma, she is an African Goddess, I'm talking straight out of Nigeria. She passed her chocolate skin, jet black hair and almond eyes down to every one of her offspring, except me. We got our curvy figures and plump butts from my Papas' side. So, it was only right that every boy in my school and on the block wanted me one of the Harris women on their arm. I personally wasn't interested, so I didn't pay them any attention. One because my Papa would kill me and two, because my heart was already taken.

Antwan Knight had stolen my heart at the tender age of sixteen. With dreads, down to his belt buckle and gray eyes that touched my soul when he looked at me. I fell in love with him the first time our eyes meet. Everyone in the hood called him Ace and he is my cousin Lil Ray's best friend. He is quiet, only spoke when necessary, but when he did people listened. Unlike my cousin, he was not flashy at all. Everyone knew that he was getting money, but looking at him you couldn't tell. I remember my Papa saying that's one of the things he loved about him. When my Papa promoted Lil Ray to running his own block, Ace was his right-hand man. Even though they were only seventeen years old, they handled business better than most grown men in the hood. To tell you the truth, at first I didn't pay any Ace any attention, he was like family, I always looked at him like a cousin.

One Saturday night Tan and I went to our home-girl house party up the block from my house. We were chilling against the wall vibeing, when I spotted Lil Ray and Ace walk through the door. Ace walked over to me, grabbed my hand, and whispered in my ear asking me to step outside. He had never really said two words to me so I was shocked. I looked at my cousin Tan for answers and she just shrugged her shoulders and continued dancing. He led me outside away from the loud noise of music and teenage laughter. Still holding my hand, he asked me to walk with him to the park. I didn't know what was up so I just kept quiet. We walked in silence for about ten minutes before he finally said something.

"Look, I've been pepping you for a while now and I'm crushing on you hard" he said.

I was at a loss for words, I didn't know how to respond. Finally, I said "My cousin and my Papa would kill us if we started dating."

He chuckled "Don't worry about that I got that handled."

"Oh, you got that handled?" I laughed as I sat in a one swing and he sat in the other.

"Yeah I do." He responded seriously.

He stared at me for a few minutes and then turned me to face him and said "Once you are mine I'm never letting you go, I'm going to take care of you forever believe dat."

We locked eyes and I felt my world change instantly. We sat and talked for hours until I realized it was close to my curfew. Ace knew how my Papa was about me so he walked me home and kissed me on the cheek.

The next day I walked to my grandparents' house as soon as I got dressed. When I walked in the front door I could hear men's voices in the kitchen. I stood next to the entryway and peeked in making sure not to be seen. To my surprise, Ace was sitting at my grandmas' kitchen table. My Papa was at the head of table and my cousin Lil Ray was seated directly across from Ace.

"Sir I know Jazzy is very important to you, and out of respect for you and your family I want to come to you and ask for your permission to date your granddaughter." Ace said.

I was in shock and scared for Ace at the same time. I just knew my Papa was about to flip the table over and choke the shit out of him.

"Nigga are you serious? That's my little cousin yo!" Lil Ray shouted.

"Shut up Ray!" Big John yelled "I got this!"

He looked Ace square in the eyes for what seemed like an eternity. I could feel my heart beating in my ears and my palms getting sweaty. I know my Papa like a book, he was getting ready to dig in Ace's ass. He lit his cigar and spoke in a voice so low I could barely hear him.

"I've watched you grow into a brilliant young man. You handle yourself in these streets better then niggas twice your age. I also take great pride in knowing that I've taught Jazzy well, she knows how to handle herself. Just know that Jazzy is like my left lung, I can't function without her. The first time she come to me and say she so much as broke a nail and you're responsible your body will be at the bottom of the Yadkin River." He declared.

I couldn't believe my ears. I had mixed feelings of excitement and nervousness. I heard my grandmother bedroom door opening so I got my ass out of there quick. I knew if I was caught ease dropping that would be my ass. I ran outside and walked around the block. By the time, I got back all three of them were gone. I chilled with my grandma for a little while then I headed home. When I got to my house Ace was sitting on my porch waiting. From that day forward we were inseparable.

CHAPTER 2

I spotted Tan walking toward me with the biggest grin on her face. Her ass was always scheming up some shit. But I was always down for whatever. I couldn't let my cousin get in trouble alone, right?

"You want to skip 7th period?" she asked beaming.

"Hell Yeah! I hate Social Studies any way. What's the move?" I exclaimed.

"We can go to my house; you know my dad still on the block he won't be home til late." She answered quickly.

So just like that we walked out the front door and walked to her house. As soon as we walked through the door I got a text message.

"Damn I forgot to let Ace know I was dipping. That's probably him." I stated reaching for my cell in my purse. Tan looked at me and rolled her eyes.

"That nigga got you wrapped around his finger." She snickered

"What bitch? Are you jealous?" I countered as I dialed his number. I didn't see the nasty look she gave me as I walked in the kitchen while waiting on Ace to pick up the phone.

"Yo What up?" Ace answered.

"Hey boo, what's up?" I responded.

"Where you at baby? I was looking for you after class, someone told me you and Tan dipped." He sounded concerned.

"Yeah, we decided not to go to 7th period, we're at Tans house now." I replied.

"You know I hate when you skip class baby. That shit is whack. Don't be   following Tan ass, she gonna get yall fucked up if Big John find out." He exclaimed.

I knew he was telling the truth. My Papa would ring both our necks if he were to find out we skipped class AGAIN. I wouldn't be in as much trouble as Tan though. I get straight A's in all my classes. But Tan on the other hand, that bitch hated school and her grades showed it.

"You're right baby. But I wasn't feeling well so I needed to come lay down." I lied.

"You ok? You need me to come get you or bring you something?" he asked with concern.

I wanted to see him so I quickly responded "Yeah come scoop me."

I hung up the phone and nearly hit the floor when I turned around and Tan was standing behind me with her arms folded across her chest.

"Got damn heifer. What the fuck? You ear hustling?" I laughed as I put my phone in my back pocket.

"So, you leaving?" she asked with a straight face.

"Yeah Ace on the way to pick me up. I'm gonna chill with him until my Mama gets home." I responded.

"Yo ass always wit Ace, damn we don't even chill no more." She threw back at me.

"We can chill this weekend I promise." I said. I leaned in and kissed her on the cheek and begin to gathered my things. The school is literally a block away so Ace would be there in no time.

"Mmmmhmmm" was her response as he pulled in the driveway and beeped the horn.

She went and stood by the window and looked out.

"When that nigga gonna get a new whip? I mean damn he still driving that beat-up maxima. It aint like he don't got the money." She asked.

I laughed and said "Bitch why you all in my mans' pocket? Worry bout what yo nigga driving.... ooops I forgot u don't got one!" I yelled as I rushed out the door before she could respond.

I jumped in the front seat of Aces 1992 grey Nissan Maxima. I kissed him on the cheek as he backed out of Tans' driveway. Tan is always clowning on Ace.

She always got something to say about his car and the way he dresses. But that's what I love about him, the fact that he is not flashy. He is one of the highest paid dope boys in my hood but he looks like a regular nigga. He gets up and goes to school every day, and makes good grades and will be graduating this year. He drives a regular car not some big ass Benz or BMW, nor does he wear a lot of expensive labels or jewelry. He hates a lot of attention so he stays low key. We have been together for almost a year and I swear I love him increasingly each day.

"Yo ass don't look sick to me. I knew yo ass was shooting me some bullshit" He said laughing.

I couldn't do anything but laugh because I was caught.

"Where you wanna go baby? We can chill at my house and watch some T.V. I'll cook your greedy ass some lunch." I said.

"Naw lets go to my crib, I got to finish my English paper before I hit the block later, you can still cook a nigga some lunch though!" he said with a wide grin on his face.

Ace is the only child of his mother Kim. His father was killed when we were about 9 years over a damn dice game. After his daddy died Ace's mother started working for my grandfather Towns to make sure that she could keep food on the table for young son. Ace always hated how Towns would treated his mother, and hated his mother even more for taking it. So, Ace spent most of his time with my family at my Papa's house. He watched how Big John ran his operation and knew he wanted to be apart, so went to Big John and asked for a job. Being that my Papa trusted Ace he gave him a job as a runner, working with Lil Ray.

Ace's Mama, Kim was not to thrilled about her son working for her boss's enemy. She told him either he had to quit working for Big John or he had to leave her house. He packed everything he owned and went to live with Lil Ray and his Mama. He stayed with them for about a year until he paid a crackhead to put an apartment in her name for him. He has been living on his own ever since. His Mama no longer works for Towns because just like my dad she fell victim to her environment and started smoking crack. Now she is living pillar to post and doing whatever for her next hit. Ace treats her as if she is a stranger.

One day while at my Papa's house Ace witnessed one of Big Johns workers stealing from him. Instead of running straight to Big John and telling him, he waited and set the worker up. He knew he couldn't go to Big John with some he says bullshit. So, Ace marked one of the packages of cocaine and waited for the worker to take it. He then went to Big John and let him know what was up. Big John immediately gathered up his goons and with Ace right by his side paid the thief a surprise visit at his home. They didn't even knock on the door when they arrived, instead Big john used his size 14 foot and kicked the door in the door in. The worker was sitting in the living room naked with two prostitutes.

"Well! Well! Looks like somebody's having a party!" Big John sang as he walked into the shabby apartment.

"What's up John. What's going on?" The worker trembled.

"I'm a little offended. You having a party and didn't invite me." He replied.

"Aww man you know it aint like that. I'm just trying to take the edge off." The worker lied shaking.

"From the looks of things, I'm hosting." Big john chuckled as he pointed to the dope on the table.

The worker didn't say anything, he just sat there, eye wide and trembling. The two prostitutes were huddled together in a corner shaking like a leaf.

"There are two things I can't stand, a liar and a thief." Big John announced as he sat on the torn leather couch. "You know what this mean don't you?" He asked.

"Come on now John...." The bullet hitting him in between the eyes stopped him mid-sentence.

Everyone looked at Ace who was standing there with a Berretta M9, pointing directly at the worker.

Without a word the 2 goons both sent a single shot to each of the vibrating hookers in the corner.

"That's what I'm talking bout!" Big John exclaimed. "Get right down to business. Let's go!" he said as he stood from the door to exit, Ace and the 2 goons following his lead.

My Papa was so impressed that that from that he promoted Ace to one of his General and gave him his own block to run, he has been running it ever since.

It took us no time to get to Ace's apartment in Kernersville, a little town right outside Winston Salem. I cooked us some hot wings and fries while he finished his English paper. After we ate I knocked my homework out while Ace did his daily work out. He then took a shower while I cleaned up the kitchen and picked him out something to wear. He stepped out the bathroom wearing nothing but a towel as I was ironing his clothes. He walked up and hugged me from behind kissing me on my neck. I could feel his dick getting hard against my butt.

He whispered in my ear "Thank you for lunch baby" and kissed me on my cheek.

I turned to face him, "No problem baby, you know I got to make sure you eat good" I replied kissing him.

"I know something else I want to eat." He implied with a devilish grin and grabbed my ass.

"Ace baby stop playing." I said and lightly pushed him away.

"I aint playing with you girl" he said pulling me back towards him and kissing my neck.

"Baby we have talked about this. That's a big step I aint ready to take. I want it to be right." I expressed.

"I know baby, but we have been together almost a year. I have been in love with you since the first time I laid eyes on you. How much more right can it get?" he asked sincerely.

"I know Ace, but I want my first time to be special. I just need a little more time baby." I responded almost apologetic.

Ace looked defeated, "Ok baby. But you can't keep coming to my house looking all sexy, cooking and cleaning for a nigga, taking care of me and shit. That shit turns me on." He said "Besides a nigga getting blue balls." He laughed as he grabbed his clothes off the ironing board to get dressed. He let his towel drop to the floor looking me in my eyes as if he were trying to bait me.

"Damn he sexy as hell" I thought as I walked into the living room to gather my books. I know Ace is getting tired of waiting, but I just ain't ready yet. I see how them little THOTS at school be jocking his ass. I knew it's just a matter of time before some bullshit happens. As Tan says "He's a man they have needs." But she has been fucking since we were 12 years old so of course she would say that. That just ain't me.

I looked at the time on my phone, it was almost 8 o'clock, my mother would be home soon and I needed to beat her there. Ace got dressed and dropped me off at home. I immediately did my chores and took a shower. I was laying my clothes out for school when Cyn knocked on my bedroom door and walked straight in as she always does.

"Damn, you could at least wait until I say come in!" I said as she plopped her ass on top of the clothes I had laid out on my bed.

"What's up sis? I see you and Tan dipped from school today. Papa gonna kick y'all ass." She said laughing.

"Well, Papa ain't gonna find out." I responded as I snatched my shirt from under her.

"Too late! He already knows! The block was hot, police kept riding so Uncle Troy came home early and caught Tan. She snitched on yo ass." Cyn exclaimed, still fucking laughing like the shit was funny.

"Damn that bitch Tan can't hold water!" I said aloud.

Cyn could see the look of terror on my face. I knew my Papa was gonna get in my ass for skipping and he would be coming to our house any minute. She laughed again and said "You better get your story together; you know he on the way." as she walked out the door.

Every night my Papa would bring the money he made for the day to my house so I can count it before I went to bed. He has safes in each of my sisters' rooms as well as mine. He never kept money in his house just in case someone tried to rob him. Once a week I would empty two of the safes and give the money to my Mama to be deposited into varies money market accounts which are all under the businesses names. My Papa and I are the ONLY people that know the codes to the safes, not even my grandmother.

I heard our front door open and my Papa's voice filled the air.

"JAZZELL NECOLE! Come here!" he yelled as he closed the door after my Mama stepped inside. I rushed to the living room. I knew if he called my name twice I would in more trouble. My Papa pulled the kitchen chair out and motioned for me to it down, of course I obeyed.

"Where's your sister?" He asked. Before I could respond Cyn was coming up the hall with the currency counter

"I'm here Papa" she said as she hurriedly placed the counter on Mamas' glass dining room table and headed back down the hall. She knew to keep her ass out of the line of fire. Papa placed two duffle bags on the floor and sat directly across from me.

"Look at me Jazzell." He said.

I looked up and directly in his eyes. One thing that my Papa hated is for someone to not look him in his face while conversing.

"How many times have we had this conversation about skipping school?" he asked.

I was about to respond but he cut me off "Shut Up Jazzell! I will let you know when it's your time to speak."

I kept my mouth closed.

"I didn't work this hard to build this life for us for y'all knuckle ass head kids to tear it down. One wrong move on the chess board and it's over. There is a reason I stress education, I'm not just talking just to hear myself talk."

I remained silent.

"They can come in here and take everything we own, but what they can't take is your mind, your intelligence. You are already a woman of color and you are a Harris, that's strikes one and two. Don't let them give you a third strike." he stated.

A simple nod was my response.

"Do you know what I do for a living? What your uncles and cousins and I do EVERY day to make this family successful?" He asked.

I didn't know if I should respond so I nodded again and kept my lips sealed tight.

"I do this now so that yall don't have to later. But to maintain success you must be educated. Not just street smart but academically as well. Those with knowledge are feared, those without knowledge are controlled."

I have heard him say these words a million times. But I sat there and listened.

"I do so much wrong in these streets I need yall to do right." He softened a little bit as he got up to sit beside me. He grabbed my hand and said "I just want what's best for yall baby girl." He kissed me on the cheek.

I looked at him and asked "Can I speak now?"

He burst into laughter. "Yes Jazzy. You can speak" he said as he unzipped one of the duffle bags and emptied its contents on the table.

"Papa I am doing everything right, I am graduating early, I'm not out there being fast, no babies, I mind my manners and do everything that is asked of me. It was only one class Papa." I said with sorrow in my voice.

"I know Jazzy. One class turns into 2 then 3. Besides Tans' ass need to be in EVERY class assigned to her plus a few more. We both know that school is not her strong point." He chuckled a little. "Look you have a month left, can you promise me that you won't skip anymore classes and leave Atkins High School with grace and dignity?"

"I promise Papa." I smiled and kissed him on the cheek.

"Good girl! Now let's count this shmoney, I got a hot date with this nice little African bombshell." He said with a grin. I could do nothing but laugh. We had all the money counted and locked away by 11 and I went straight to bed. But before I closed my eyes I sent Tan a nasty text message. She is going to hear my mouth in the morning.

CHAPTER 3

"Yo what's poppin Ray? Where the hell is everybody at?" Ace said as he looked around the deserted block.

"Shit, 12 been riding all damn day. Them little young niggas done made the block hot doing dumb shit" Lil Ray responded before hitting his blunt.

Ace looked at him like he was nuts "Well what the fuck you still doing out here? You know how Big John is, once you see too much police movement he wants shit shut down."

Lil Ray laughed and said "I ain't making no noise, I just aint ready to go home yet."

As they were talking Juice pulled up. Juice was from our block and grew up with Lil Ray and Ace. His real name is Duwan Burton but everyone calls him Juice because back in the day when they all used to play for Pop Warner, Juice was the running back. My Papa and his friends would say he ran like O.J Simpson so they started calling him Juice and it stuck. He played ball all the way up until his Junior year of high school, had college scoots checking for him and everything. His only problem was he couldn't leave the streets alone. He seen how his homeboys was getting money and he wanted to get money too.

Being that they all grew up together Lil Ray and Ace decided to put him on and let him work for them. The thing is, he aint built for the shit. One night while they were all on the block doing what they do. A car that they had never seen before pulled up to the trap. Some corny looking black dude got out and walked up to them asking about buying some coke. Both Lil Ray and Ace told the unknown man the same thing.

"I don't know what you talking about."

But Juice dumbass chasing every dollar said "I got you, what you need?" And walked the stranger down the block and around the corner to serve him. Ace and

Lil Ray were both pissed. When Juice returned, Ace cursed him out and demanded he leave the block. He and Lil Ray decided it was best to shut it down for the night as well. After they left Juice came back to the block to make some more money.

Later that night Ace got a phone call from one of his young boys saying that Juice was locked up. Turns out the corny looking black dude was an undercover cop. When Juice went back to the block the strange dude came back for more coke. As Juice was serving him, the police ran up on him and locked him up. Ace sent his bail bondsman to bond him out the following day, hired Juice a lawyer and never fucked with him again on business.

Juice now had a criminal record so college ball was no longer in his future. When Ace stopped suppling him, Juice quit school and started working for Towns. Ever since then he and Ace have had some animosity. They kept it cordial on the strength of them growing up together and the fact that Juice knew better then to cross that line with Ace.

"What's good fam?" Juice said as he exited the car.

"Not shit. What's up with you?" Lil Ray responded dapping Juice up.

Juice looked at Ace, "What up Ace?" he said. Ace just nodded his head and kept scrolling through his phone without even glancing up.

"What yall got going on?" Juice asked no one in particular.

"Nothing much just chillin. Bout to take it in for the night. What the hell you doing up here?" Lil Ray retorted.

"Just out, checking on a few things. I wanted to holla at you about something though Ray." He looked over at Ace hesitantly before continuing "I been getting some really good numbers on my product from Towns. I wanted to cut you in so you can make some serious dough."

Before Lil Ray could speak Ace jumped up, "Nigga you got some mother fucking nerve!" He shouted. "How the fuck you gonna bring yo ass to Big Johns block, stepping to his grandson about anything that has to do with that nigga Towns?"

Juice looked at Ace and through clenched teeth replied "Nigga I aint talking to you."

In a spilt second Ace was in Juice's face. "Well I'm talking to yo bitch ass." He said grilling Juice daring him to jump.

"Be easy Ace." Lil Ray said jumping in the middle of the two, "Look Juice you know we don't fuck with that grimy ass nigga Towns. I don't give a fuck if he was giving that shit away for free. We good over her fam."

"Exactly! So, get yo punk ass back in your ride and get the fuck from round here!" Ace exclaimed still grilling Juice. Juice just stared at Ace for a few seconds before walking away and getting in his car.

Soon as he turned out the neighborhood he made a call. "What's up boo?" she answered on the first ring.

"What's going on baby? What you doing?" Juice responded.

"Nothing much. Thinking about you." She said. Juice could hear her smiling through the phone. He knew he has her right where he wanted her.

CHAPTER 4

I was awakened by my alarm on my cell phone at 6 AM telling me it's time to get up and get ready for school. I hit snooze and laid my head back on my pillow. And just like clockwork Ace called, 6:05AM on the dot.

"Good morning baby." I answered without opening my eyes.

"Hey gorgeous. You not up yet?" Ace said wide awake.

"No, I'm getting up now. I will see you when you get here." I said hanging up and throwing myself of bed. I hated mornings. I brushed my teeth, washed my face, and got dressed. I was just sliding my Jordan's on my feet when I heard Ace blow the horn and his car door shut. He met me at the door and grabbed my book bag.

I yelled back in the house, "Cyn and Kia if yall want a ride yall better come on or else you will be on the bus."

They came running down the hall like wild animals. Ace opened each of our doors before sliding in the driver's seat. He kissed me on the cheek, looked me up and down and laughed.

"Boy what you laughing at?" I asked with a little bit of attitude.

"Damn baby, was you looking through a nigga window while I was getting dressed this morning?" he said still laughing.

I looked at his outfit and busted out laughing. We were dressed exactly alike. We both had on a red and white stripped Polo shirt some light blue Levi's and the red and white Jordan 12's.

"Great minds think alike baby." Ace said chuckling as he backed out of our drive way and headed to school.

After walking Cyn and Kia to their hallways Ace and I headed straight for my locker. There was Tan leaning against it playing on her phone.

"What up cuz? Don't yall look cute." She said with an invidious tone. I just smirked at her and proceeded to open my locker. Lil Ray walked up, gave Ace dap, and hugged me from behind.

"What's up cuz. I got those notes from Social Studies since yall ass decided to skip yesterday." He said laughing.

"Thanks boo. You know Papa dug in my ass last night too." I glaring at Tan. "Speaking of, how the fuck you gonna snitch on me like that?"

Tan sucked her teeth and said "What you mean? My dad came home early; we were caught!"

"No bitch yo ass was caught! All you had to do was take your cursing out and keep yo mouth shut." I shot back. She looked pissed off, but I didn't give a fuck.

"My bad Jaz, it won't happen again." She said looking down at the floor.

"Damn right it won't cause I aint skipping with yo ass no more. I just want to get through this last month of school without getting in anymore shit with Papa." I said just as the bell rang for first period. I kissed Ace and we all went our separate ways. Tan is my cousin and my best friend but she been on some bullshit lately.

The day flew by quickly, before I knew it the bell was ringing for the end for dismissal. I gathered my stuff and headed to Ace's car. I was surprised to see I beat him to the student parking lot. I was leaning against his car scrolling through Snapchat when I looked up and seen Tan standing in front of the school. I figured maybe Uncle Troy was picking her up to make sure she hadn't skipped. Then I see that lame nigga Juice pull up and Tan hop in the front seat.

"Why the fuck would Juice be picking Tan up from school?" I thought. Just as I was about to call her and see what's up I heard Ace voice. I looked over and he was walking out the building with Tonya Broadhurst. Tan instantly became the furthest thing on my mind. Tonya was one of the biggest hoes in the school. She had big boobs, a fat ass and long fake ass hair. She can dress her ass off, I will give her that, but the bitch can't hold a candle to me on her best day. I watched how they interacted as they made their way to the student parking lot. I noticed how she flirted with him, kept touching his arm and flipping that stiff ass Yaki weave. How she laughed at everything he said, that nigga aint that damn funny. By the time they were close to me, the look on my face could scare the devil himself. Immediately her big ass smile faded into a smirk. Ace on the other hand carried a look mixed with concerned and "oh shit" on his face.

He walked up to me and said "Hey baby, you aight?" as he kissed me on the lips.

"Bye Ace thanks for all your help" Tonya sang as she walked pass.

I just glared at her as Ace replied "No problem Tonya." He grabbed my book bag and started to walk around the car to open my door.

"What the fuck you doing with that bitch?" I said loud enough so she could hear.

Tonya had common sense, she just chuckled and kept walking to her red Honda Civic. Ace looked at me as if I had lost my mind.

"Yo get your ass in the car!" He said with his teeth clenched tight.

I stomped to the passenger side like a spoiled 2-year-old and slid in the car. Ace slammed my door and walked around to the drivers' side

"What the fuck is yo problem?" he barked as soon as he closed the door. "You know I aint with that drama shit."

"Like I said what the fuck are you doing with that bitch?" I snapped.

"She was having trouble with some calculus problems, she asked for my help. Simple. Point Blank. Period." He replied

"All the mother fuckers in y'all class she had to ask you? You should've told that hoe to google it, shit ask the teacher, that's what he there for." I was pissed off.

"Look baby there aint nothing at this school that interest me, I'm yours. You never have to worry about me cheating on you." Ace said, "But if you feel like you need to ask don't do that shit in front of mother fuckers. That's between you and me. Don't let these bitches think they can make you insecure. Then they will feel they can come in between us."

Ace was right, "I'm sorry baby." I said and gave him a kiss.

"Besides, I can't do nothing with Tonya and all that weave. That shit be shedding all over the damn classroom. You know I aint with that weave shit. I got a natural beauty, why would I cheat with something fake?" Ace looked at me and winked as he started the car and backed out of the parking spot. I blushed and laughed at the same time as we headed to my house to chill.

"You want me to make you something to eat Ace?" I asked getting up from my bed to head to the kitchen.

"No baby I am good." He replied. He was laying on the floor messing around on my laptop. Weather we were there alone or with a house full of people, my bedroom door remained open while Ace was there. Ace says it is a sign of respect to my Mama and my sisters. As I was leaving the room my cell phone rung.

"Baby can you grab that for me?" I asked and proceeded to the kitchen to get us something the drink. When I returned Ace still had my phone to his ear. I handed him a glass of juice and sat back on the bed to continue catching up on Love & Hip Hop.

"That's wild Ray, I'm going to have to get with Jazzy on that." Ace spoke into the phone. Ace talked for a few more minutes than ended the call.

"Yo babe that was Ray, he said he was riding through the hood on the way to the block to checkup on his young niggas and he seen dat nigga Juice whip parked in front of yo cousin crib." He looked at me "You know anything bout that?" he asked.

"At Tan house?" I responded shocked. "Yo I seen him picked her up from school today. I was gonna say something but it slipped my mind. What the fuck is going on?" I asked.

"Hell, if I know." Ace responded as he went back to fingering with the laptop.

I grabbed my phone, "Well I'm getting ready to find out" I said as I dialed Tans number. She didn't answer so I called right back. Again, no answer, so I sent her a text message. She had better call me back, I needed answers now. We never kept secrets from each other.

"You want something to drink Juice?" Tan said as he got up from her bed to put her robe on her naked body.

"Naw I'm cool." Juice replied reaching for his phone on the floor. He waited until Tan was out of the room before he made his call.

"Everything is going according to plan. That bitch gonna be singing in no time." He said the whomever was on the other end of the line. He ended the call just as Tan was walking through the bedroom door with a can of soda. Her dad was out of town doing a run for Big John and wasn't due home until the next morning. She sat on the edge of her bed and turned the T.V on with the remote. Her cell phone rang on the night stand,

"Babe can you hand me my phone." She asked Juice while reaching back. Juice picked her phone off the night stand and glanced at it before he tossed it across the bed to her. Tan picked up the phone looked at the caller ID and sucked her teeth and tossed it back on the bed.

"Aye you good?" Juice asked acting concerned.

"Yeah, I'm cool, it's just Jazzy. I don't feel like dealing with her right now." Tan replied. Her phone rang again; she knew it was Jazzy calling back so she didn't even bother to look at it.

"Damn baby, what happened? I thought yall was tight." Juice asked.

Tan shook her head and said "We are tight, but ever since she started fucking with that nigga Ace she been different."

The sound of Ace's name made Juice skin crawl.

"What you mean different?" He asked patting the bed beside him motioning for her to come closer. She smiled as she stood up, let her robe fall to floor exposing her naked body and climbed back in bed with him. He laid her head on his chest as he played in her hair.

"I mean, she doesn't really rock with me like that no more. It's all about Ace. They always together." Juice sat there taking it all in as Tan continued to talk. "Like today, she promised to chill with me today. But is she here? No. She probably with Ace. Laid up, NOT fuckin." Tan said shaking her head.

"What you mean NOT fucking? Ace aint hitting that?" Juice asked almost laughing.

"Naw Jazzy a virgin. She claims she wants to wait until the right time, whatever that means." Tan responded.

"Well I'll be damned" Juice thought as he laid his head against the head board. He listened to Tan complain about Jazzy a little more before he got dressed and headed to his block.

As he was leaving the hood he rode past Ace and Lil Ray on the block. He threw his hand up the to speak while he chuckled and shook his head

"Pussy ass mother fucker" He said to himself. "Your day is coming."

CHAPTER 5

I woke up to the sun shining in my window. It was a beautiful Saturday morning and there was only one way to spend it, at the mall. I hopped out the bed and jumped in the shower. It's warming up outside so I decided to wear some shorts and my Michael Kors sandals that Ace brought me. I called Tan to see if she wanted to roll with me but again she didn't answer the phone, so I decided to pop up at her house.

As I was walking through the hood I seen Lil Ray, Ace and some of the corner boys playing ball at the court. I noticed Tonya and her crew sitting on the stairs watching and giggling. I leaned against Ace's car and watched them run up and down the pavement sweating and yelling at each other.

Once Ace spotted me he called "Time Out" and ran over my way.

"Hey beautiful, where you headed?" he asked as he kissed me on the lips trying not to drip sweat on me.

"I'm gonna go holla at Tan then head over to the mall. I see you got your cheerleading squad over there" I said looking over at Tonya and her bird ass crew. She was staring at us the whole time.

Ace laughed "Aint nobody checking for those broads. You going to the mall huh? Yo pockets straight?" he asked.

"You know I'm good." I responded.

He reached in his pocket for his keys and unlocked his car doors.

"Get in right quick." He said as he opened the car door. He looked back and yelled towards the court "Aye yo give me a min" and he jogged over to the drivers' side of the car and got in. He reached in the glove box and pulled out a stack of money. He peeled off ten $100 dollar bills

"Get something to wear for tonight, we going out." He said as he handed the bills to me. I placed them neatly in my Louis Vuitton wallet and put it back in the matching purse.

"Thank you, baby." I said with a smile and kissed him on the cheek.

Lil Ray ran over to the car and knocked on the window.

"Aye we ballin or what?" he asked through the closed window.

I opened the car door to get out.

"Damn nigga you aint gonna speak with yo rude ass?" I said laughing while climbing out he car.

"Aww cuz my bad baby. I'm just ready to finishing schooling yo man on the court!" he exclaimed dribbling the ball in between his legs.

Ace and I both laughed as he locked the glove box and exited the car. "Aight baby call me when you get home, let me get back out here and finishing teaching yo cousin how to handle this ball." He said as and kissed me again before he ran back to the court. I glared back at Tonya before I walked away towards my Papa house.

I walked in the front door at my grandparents' house and found my Grandma in the kitchen at the stove cooking something that smelled heavenly. "Hey grandma, where Papa at?" I asked after I kissed her on the cheek.

"Hey baby, you hungry?" she asked.

"No ma'am" I responded

"Your Papa is in his office" she said. "I was just about to fix him a plate, you wanna take it to him for me baby?" she asked.

"Yes ma'am" I responded as I went to the sink to wash and dry my hands.

My grandma placed a plate of baked chicken, steamed cabbage, rice and gravy and a roll on a wooden serving tray. I grabbed a glass out of the cabinet and filled it with ice and sweet tea and placed it on the tray alongside the silver knife and fork that was laying on a napkin.

"Thank you, baby." My grandma said and kissed me on my forehead. I smiled as I lifted the tray and headed down the hall toward my Papa's office.

As I walked down the hall the smell of my Papa's cigar hit me in the face. I always loved that smell. The door was slightly open so I peeked my head in and smiled at him. He was sitting at his desk reading the newspaper and smoking a cigar.

He looked up at me, "Hey love bug, how is my favorite granddaughter?" he asked as I walking in the door.

"I'm great Papa, you ready to eat old man??" I asked as I sat the tray on his desk and kissed him on his forehead.

He laughed "Old man huh?' he said looking at his plate. He inhaled the intoxicating aroma, "your grandma sure knows how to keep a smile on my face," he exclaimed, "You not eating baby?" He asked.

Just as I was about to respond my grandma walked in with a second serving tray with a steaming hot plate of food on it.

"Yes, she is. Jazzy come have lunch with your Papa." She said as she placed the tray on the opposite side of the desk and pulled the chair out for me to have a seat.

Even though I wasn't hungry it would be disrespectful not to eat at this point so I sat down. We both bowed our heads and gave thanks for the meal placed in front of us. When I opened my eyes my grandma had slipped out the room and my Papa and I were alone. We randomly chatted about school and my grades as we ate our food.

Then he asked, "What's going on with you and your cousin? I noticed that the dynamic duo has become a solo act." Big John said while slicing into his chicken.

I knew it was coming.

"Papa I don't know," I responded shaking my head, "she has been real distant lately. I called her twice just today and no answer."

My Papa was quiet for a second then he looked at me

"Are you sure its Tan that's been distant?" he asked with a raised eyebrow.

The question confused me. "What do you mean?" I asked.

"Well I've notice that ever since you and Ace started dating you have been missing in action, hell you barely come over here anymore." He stated.

I didn't say anything.

"Jazzy I raised yall to be tight, to always stick together no matter what or who." He said "I understand Ace is your boyfriend and he is a good man, I am not negating that. But family is family. Don't change up."

"I understand Papa; I am gonna make it right I promise." I uttered.

"What you got planned for the rest of the day?" he probed.

"Going to the mall, do some shopping. I am going to stop by Tan's to see if she wants to roll with me." I answered barely nibbling on my food.

"Good! Yo pockets straight?" he inquired.

I chuckled a little bit before responded. "Yes Papa. I'm good."

He stood up from his desk, reached in his pocket and pulled out a wad of money. He counted out $2000 and handed it to me.

"Make sure yall make a day of it. Tell Ace yall can go out next Saturday." He stated.

"How did you know...." I started to ask.

My Papa threw his hand up to stop me "I know everything Jazzell." He remarked with a smile. We both laughed and finished our lunch.

As I walked out of my grandparents' house I called Tan on my cell phone, again no answer. I jumped on Facebook to see if she had posted anything lately. I noticed she had just posted a status a half hour ago.

"What the fuck?" I whispered to myself as I made my way towards her house.

When I got there my uncle Troy was sitting on the front porch supervising one of the neighborhood crackheads washing his car.

"Hey niecey!" He exclaimed as I reached the top of the driveway.

"Hey there Unc, how are u?" I asked as I hugged him

"If I was any finer I'd be china!" he said and we both laughed.

"Is Tan home?" I asked.

"Yeah she in there." He replied nodding toward the door.

"Thanks, Unc." I said walking through the front door. I went straight down the hall towards Tan's bedroom door. As I was about to knock I could hear her talking on the phone.

"Yeah baby, that's cool. We can hang out tonight. I will just tell my dad I'm spending the night at Jazzy house." I heard her say to whoever she was on the phone with.

"She always scheming" I said to myself before knocking on the door.

"Just a minute dad I'm getting dressed." She yelled through the door.   "Aye let me call you right back." She said to the caller.

She opened the door and the look on her face was priceless.

"What up cuz?" I asked as I walked in her room. She just stood at the door like she was stuck to the floor. I sat on the edge of her bed and looked at her.

"Damn Tan what's up, I been calling you, why you ducking me?" I asked.

She rolled her eyes closed the door, "I just been busy that's all." She said as she walked across the room and sat at her desk.

"Busy? With what bitch? And who the hell was you on the phone with?" I ask looking at her sideways.

She didn't say anything, just looked at the floor.

"Tan what's up?" I asked again getting louder

"Look don't be coming over here questioning me. What the hell you doing here anyway? What Ace busy so you decided to slide through as if you aint been missing for weeks? Miss me with the bullshit Jazzy!" she yelled back.

"Look I know I been stuck up under Ace a lot lately and putting you on the back burner. I promise that's gonna change. We family, we got to stick together, no matter what or who." I said sincerely.

Tan said nothing just continue to look at the floor as if all the answers were stitched in the carpet.

"Let's have a girl's day, you know like we used to, do some shopping, get our nails done, the whole nine.

She hesitated as if she wasn't sure if I was serious. I reached in my purse and grabbed all the money out of my wallet.

"Bitch is you rocking with me or what?" I said waving $8000 dollars in the air.

Tan laughed, stood up and walked over to her dresser. She opened the top drawer and pulled out a stack of money.

"You aint saying shit! Let's go spend this dough!" she said. "Just give me 10 minutes to get dressed." And she ran to get in the shower.

"*Where the fuck did she get that money?*" I thought to myself as I flipped on the TV and waited.

After Tan got dressed, we caught an Uber to Hanes Mall and shopped until we were tired. We then went to the nail salon and ended the day at my Mama's shop so Tan could get her hair washed and flat ironed. When we were done, we decided to go back to my house, order some Chinese food and chill. I couldn't wait to get in my pajamas, pig out and talk shit with my cousin like old times. My Mama shop is right at the top of our block so we walked to my house. As we were walking up the driveway, Tan got a phone call. She looked at the caller ID, looked at me and pressed the ignore button. Before she could put her cell back in her purse, it rang again, and again she ignored the call, only this time she turned the ringer off afterwards.

"Who is that?" I asked.

"Damn noisy! None of yo business." She laughed trying to avoid the question.

"So, that's how it is?" I asked turning the key to unlock the front door. We went straight to the bedroom dropped our bags and head toward to kitchen. I threw some popcorn in the microwave as Tan poured us both a glass of juice. Cyn and Kia were at my aunts' house as they were every weekend and my Mama works late at the shop on the weekends, so we had the house to ourselves.

We sat in the living room and chatted about nothing as we watched TV. We were laughing at the woman of Atlanta Housewives when there was a knock on the door. We both jumped up and looked out the window, Aces' car was parked in the driveway.

Tan sucked her teeth and glared at me, "I guess it's time for me to go home."

I rolled my eyes, "Heifer shut up yo ass up and order us some Chinese food. I will get rid of him." I retorted walking to the door.

"What you want?" she asked brightly as she reached for her cell.

"The usual" I was responded opening the door to let Ace in. "What's up baby? What you doing here?" I asked.

He looked over at Tan "Can I talk to you right quick? I won't be long I promise."

"Of course," I said.

"I'll be right back." I threw at Tan as we were walked down the hall to my bedroom. As soon as we were behind closed doors Ace began to empty his pockets on my bed.

"Yo put this dough up for me, I will come get it later tonight. You know I don't feel comfortable with all this money on me while on the block and I don't got time to drive all the way to my house."

"Ok" I said as I pulled the small safe he kept at my house from under my bed "But can you come get it in the morning? Me and Tan having a girls' night tonight."

Ace paused for a second and looked at the door. "Yo you heard that?" He asked.

"Heard what?" I looked confused.

"It sounded like someone was at the door." Another pause, "Maybe I'm tripping" he said shrugging his shoulders. We proceeded to put the money in the safe, lock it and slid it back under the bed.

"Thanks bae," he said kissing me. We exited the room and I walked him to the door.

"Aight Tan you can have her back since she kicking me out." He said laughing "Enjoy yall girls' night."

Tan just threw her hand up and continued placing our food order. After locking the door behind Ace I wrapped my hair and took a shower so I can be on chill mode when my food arrived, Tan did the same. She was just walking in the living room in her pajamas when the delivery guy knocked on the door.

We ate and watched Paid in Full for the millionth time.

"I miss us chilling like this." Tan said, "We never get to hang out no more." She looked sad.

"I know Tan; I promise things are gonna be like they used to be." I replied.

"What happened to us tho? You flipped on me for Ace. I mean he cool and all but damn Jaz you don't even fuck with me no more." She uttered.

"Nothing happened, I just like spending time with Ace, that's my boo. I mean you know how it is." I responded.

"Yeah I know." She claimed just as her phone was ringing. She looked at the caller ID and just as before she ignored the call.

"Speaking of, who the hell been blowing you up all damn day, and why are you curving them?" I asked suspiciously.

Tan hesitated before she spoke, "Its nobody, this dude I been fucking with, nothing major."

"Is it Juice?" I asked. She looked at me in shock, her eyes wide.

"I saw him pick you up from school the other day and Ray say his car was parked at your house all that afternoon. What up wit that?" I questioned.

"Damn yall all in aint yall?" she asked laughing.

"Naw bitch spill the tea, I want to know everything." I said.

I don't know why Tan was being so secretive, we told each other everything.

"Yeah we been messing around for about a month or so. He's' cool, kind of lame but he been breaking bread so I just been entertaining him," She laughed, "But it ain't nothing serious."

"Entertaining him? So, you done fucked him? After only a month? Come on now you know better." I said almost in a motherly tone.

Tan got heated "See that's why I didn't want to tell yo ass! You always judging!" she yelled.

"Naw baby girl I aint judging I'm just saying its quick." I responded, "Get out yo feelings, if I can't be straight up with you, my cousin, my best friend, then our bond aint what I thought it was." I threw back.

"Well like I said it aint nothing serious, and besides I aint no prude like yo stuck up ass. I like fucking. You know this, I know this it's no secret." She declared.

I felt like she wasn't telling me the whole truth but I decided not to pry any further, at least I knew were the money came from. I really had no one to blame but myself, if I was around more than I would know.

"You still aint gave that nigga Ace no butt yet huh?" she asked laughing hard, "that nigga probably done forgot how to fuck waiting on yo ass! Keep on making him wait, I'm sure some thot just waiting to remind him."

I just looked at her and then looked at the floor. She was probably right, but Ace wouldn't do me like that, or would he?

CHAPTER 6

"Yo Ace what's the plan for tonight?" Lil Ray asked, while chilling on the block playing around with the dice.

"Shit, its whatever. Jazzy and Tan having a girls' night so I'm free." He responded "What you tryin to do?"

"Tonya having a party down in Creekwood, You wanna slide through?" Ray solicited.

Ace thought about it for a second "You know your cousin would be heated if I went, she can't stand Tonya's' ass!" Ace laughed.

"It's just a party, damn Jazzy will be aight, it aint like you trying to fuck the girl." Ray tried to reason.

"You right, and I'm board as hell. Fuck it! I'm gonna go home and jump in the shower I will meet you at yo crib bout 10 and we can roll out." Ace said giving in.

Everything in him was telling him not to fucking go, but against his better judgment he went home and got dressed.

They arrived at Tonya's' party around 10:30, and it was lit. Everyone from school was there and even some people from the hood. Ace and Lil Ray were chilling against the wall when Tonya spotted them.

"Damn Ace is here; I didn't expect him to come." Tonya said to her home girl Cheryl.

"And he with my boo!" Cheryl screeched with excitement. Her and Lil Ray have been flirting with each other since freshman year, Cheryl been waiting on Ray to make the first move and ask her out but he never did, he just flirted a little bit and kept it moving.

"I'm surprised that bitch Jazzy let him come out, you know she got that nigga on a short leash. Hell, I don't blame her, that nigga sexy as hell" Tonya said glaring at Ace seductively, "and he got paper." Tonya added.

"Girl I know right! That bitch pussy must be made of gold cause Ace won't even look at another chick." Cheryl responded laughing.

"Let's go over there." Tonya insisted pulling Cheryl by the arm.

"Damn how yall gone come to my party and don't even speak? How rude." Tonya said jokingly when she walked up to the two of them.

"Oh, what up Tonya, we didn't even see you when we came in." Lilray said. "How you doing Cheryl, you looking good baby." Cheryl blushed as he grabbed her hand and moved her closer to him to whisper in her ear.

Ace looked at Tonya and asked "You want something to drink I got a little bottle in the car." Tonya nodded and he led the way out of the party towards LilRay car. He popped the trunk and pulled out a fifth of Jose' Curevo Gold.

"Oh shit, I should have grabbed us some cups." Tonya uttered.

"Girl you better turn this bottle up, stop playing." Ace laughed and took a swig out of the bottle before handing it over to her. Tonya looked around before doing the same. She took another drink before handing it back.

"Do you think Ray would mind if I sit on his car?" she asked,

"Naw you good." Ace responded and took another drink from the bottle. Tonya jumped on the trunk of the car and reached out for the bottle.

"You better slow down, the Jose' aint nothing to play wit." Ace joked and handed her the bottle.

"I'm a big girl, I can handle it." She said and took a long swig of the potent poison. They sat in silence for a few minutes as they passed the bottle back and forth.

"I'm surprised Jazzy let you come out, everybody knows she got you on lock." Tonya taunted.

Ace snickered and said "That's what everybody knows huh?"

"Yep that's the word." Tonya retorted.

"It's not about being on lock; I just respect Jazzy. She holds me down." Ace informed.

Tonya felt a twinge of jealousy. "But damn she doesn't let you do shit." She said.

"Do shit like what?" He asked "what don't she let me do?"

"Hell, I don't know, I don't never see you out, like I said I was surprised to see you here tonight." Tonya fired back.

"Naw it's not like that. Jazzy likes to chill and I like to chill wit her that's all." He explained.

"So, what do yall do when yall "chillin" or whatever?" she asked jumping off the trunk and walking closer to Ace.

"What you mean?" he asked "We chill."

Tonya laughed, "Chill huh, what yall sit watch TV with her little sisters and shit?" She moved closer. "I bet she a prude in bed, I bet she don't let you hit it from the back, let you grab and smack her ass, hell she probably only let you hit it once a month if that." She grabbed Aces' hand and placed it on her round ass. Ace started to snatch away but he was feeling the effects of the liquor and her ass felt so good, so he gripped it hard and she let out a moan.

"You think you can handle all this baby?" she asked. Before he could answer Tonya kissed him shoving her tongue in his mouth. Her kiss felt forced, it felt artificial, it felt wrong. Ace turned his head to break their kiss and tried to step away but Tonya held on tighter.

"Look Tonya...." Ace started to say but Tonya cut him off.

"You don't have to worry about shit Ace, I promise after a night wit me you will forget all about Jazzy."

Ace looked at her like she had lost her damn mind "Tonya you cool and all but I love my girl, I can't do this." He said backing away putting some space in between them. Tonya was livid.

"What the fuck you scared of, Damn that bitch done turned you into a punk, what you scared of pussy?" She shouted, "You going this hard for a bitch that won't even suck yo dick."

It took everything in Ace not to smack the shit out of her.

"Bitch I'm trying to spare yo feelings, yo best bet is to walk the fuck away." He said calmly.

"Bitch? Who the fuck you calling a bitch?" She got louder "What nigga passes up good pussy? You gay or something? Wit'cho bitch ass!"

Before Ace could catch himself, he blanked out on Tonya "Good pussy? Community pussy aint good pussy to me. I like my pussy clean, untainted. Not passed around to every nigga in school. You couldn't see my bitch on her worst day and I make sure she stunts on all yall hoes every chance she gets! Dizzy ass broad, I'd be a fool to let you anywhere near my dick"

He walked away leaving Tonya looking like her words were stuck in her throat because she couldn't say shit. Ace decided not to go back in the party, instead he started walking back to the block, he was steaming.

"I knew shouldn't have brought my ass to this damn party" he said to himself. He thought about calling Jazzy to tell her what happened but he decided against it.

Tonya stormed back in the party pissed off and embarrassed. As soon as she walked through the door she bumped into LilRay.

"Aye yo Tonya where my boy at?" he asked.

"Hell, if I know, fuck Ace!" she barked and pushed past him almost knocking him over. Ray and Cheryl looked at each other baffled, Cheryl ran to catch up with Tonya as Ray reached in his pocket for his cell phone.

Ace answered on the first ring "Yo what up?"

"Where you at nigga?" Ray asked.

"I'm walking up the block headed back to the hood. This ain't my scene I had to dip." Ace responded.

"I'm on my way to scoop you." Ray said, by this time he was in his car turning the key in the ignition. He sped out of the parking lot and a was pulling up on Ace in no time.

"Yo what the fuck happened?" Ray asked as soon as Ace closed the door. Ace hesitated about telling Ray, even though they were boys he was Jazzy's cousin first, aint no telling how he would react.

"Nothing man, that bitch throwed off." He said "It's still early, what we bout to get into?" Ace wanted to change the subject as quick as possible.

"Shit, I'm feeling lucky, let's go to the card house." Ray said.

"I'm cool with that. I wouldn't mind takin a motha fukas money." Ace returned laughing.

A knock at my bedroom door startled me out of my sleep. I looked around the room and over at Tan snoring beside me.

"Come in" I said to whoever was on the other side of the door. My Mama cracked the door and peeked in.

"I'm bout to cook some breakfast, yall want some pancakes?" she asked.

"Yes ma'am" I responded "You need some help ma?" I asked hoping she would say no.

"Naw baby, your sister helping me." She said and closed the door.

I reached over to the night stand to get me cell phone, it was already 10AM.

"Damn Ace aint called. That's strange." I shrugged and put my phone back. I got up, went to the use the bathroom and brush my teeth. By the time I got back to my room Tan was up, laying in the bed playing on her phone.

"Damn bitch you aint gone brush yo teeth before you get on Facebook?" I asked joking.

"Whatever fish. Damn I forgot all about Tonya's' party last night. It looks like that shit was lit." She said.

"Bitch please! You know damn well I wasn't going to that hoes party. Bitch probably got a house full of fucking roaches." I spat.

"Well I guess Ace don't mind roaches." She said turning her phone toward me.

"WHAT THE FUCK?" I shouted grabbing my phone.

"JAZZELL! Watch yo mouth!" my Mama shouted from the kitchen. I threw my hand over my mouth being that I had quickly forgotten where I was. I scrolled through Tans Facebook timeline in disbelief, there was a few pictures of Ace and Ray standing against the wall and few of him and Tonya standing outside, Ace was leaning against Rays' car and Tonya was sitting on the trunk. I could feel my blood start to boil. I snatched my phone from the night stand and began to dial Aces' number.

"What you doing?" Tan asked looking puzzled.

"I'm bout to call this nigga and see what the fuck is up. What you think?" I answered looking at Tan as if she had two heads.

She jumped up and snatched my phone out my hand

"Bitch is you crazy? What you gonna call him and curse him out and then what?" she asked.

I stood there with a blank stare, I was lost.

She smacked her teeth and shook her head,

"Got damn bitch haven't I taught yo ass anything?" she asked rhetorically. "Girl you hold the power, he doesn't know that you know. Sit back and watch this shit play out."

I sat on my bed and thought for a second, Tan might be right.

"Ok I'm going to call him and feel him out I aint gonna say nothing." I said.

"Mmmmhhhmmm." Tan uttered skeptically hand me my phone. She stood up, grabbed her towel, and headed to the door. Before leaving she looked back at me.

"You know what type of nigga you got, if he come out and tell you without you asking then you good money, if he keeps it from you then you might want to ask yourself why? Like Papa always say withholding the truth is just like a lying. Besides your birthday is tomorrow, you don't break up with your boyfriend the day before your birthday, you get the gift first." She laughed trying to lighten the mood walked out the room.

I was left sitting on the edge of my bed, phone in my hand, scared to see what the outcome would be.

Ace looked at his phone for the millionth time since last night. He and Ray stayed at the card house till 5:30 AM and he couldn't sleep when he finally got home. He didn't know what to do about Tonya. He knew Jazzy would be 38 hot when she finds out he even went to the party. And she's gonna find out, there was no way around it. Shit she probably already knew, everyone they knew was there and it was already all over Facebook, Snapchat, and Instagram by now. But that was the least of his worries, Jazzy wouldn't be mad for long about that. But if ANYBODY saw, or if Tonya ole petty ass told anybody what happened then he was in deep shit. Ace didn't know what to do, should he tell her and get it over with or let it play out.

"Fuck it, I'm just gonna call and feel her out." he said to himself as he dialed her number and waited for her to answer.

"Hello" Jazzy answered on the first ring.

She knows Ace thought, "Hey gorgeous, what you doing?" Ace said trying to sound normal.

"Hey boo, nothing much just bout to eat some breakfast. What you up to?" she asked.

Maybe she doesn't know Ace retreated. "Nothing much just getting up" Ace replied.

"Why you didn't call me last night? What did you end up doing?" Jazzy quizzed.

Ace panicked a little bit, "Ray and I went to Tonya's party for a minute, then we went and played cards till bout 5:30." He couldn't lie to her but he didn't have the balls to tell her the whole truth.

Jazzy was silent for a second then she said "That's what's up, I seen that on Facebook. How was it?" she asked.

"It was cool we wasn't there long. I won $2600 at the card table last night though." Ace pronounced, he couldn't feel her out she was being too nonchalant.

"That's what's up" was all she said back.

"You wanna hang out later? I can come scoop you around 6. We can start celebrating your birthday early." Ace raised, hoping she would agree.

"Yeah that's cool, I will be ready at 6." Jazzy responded.

"Aight baby, see you later. I love you." Ace spoke into the phone.

"Yeah me too." was Jazzys' comeback before ending the call.

Ace didn't know what the fuck to think. Jazzy was being too fucking calm about this whole thing. Maybe she not mad, Ace tried to reason. He would just have to see when they are face to face.

"Damit Man!" Ace yelled to himself in the empty apartment.

I hung up the phone and looked at Tan, "Well...." What did he say?" Tan asked.

"He said him and LilRay went to the party for a Lilbit then went to the card house for the rest of the night." I explained.

"Well there you go, he told you without you asking. You good. Right?" Tan inquired.

"I don't know Tan, it's some fishy shit going on. I feel it." I answered.

"Girl you tripping! That nigga could have easily lied but he told you the truth. Take it for what it is and keep it moving." Tan justified.

"I feel you. Maybe I'm just paranoid." I voiced.

Tan continued "But I will tell you one thing, you keep making that nigga wait it's only a matter of time before he starts seeking elsewhere. Like the saying goes, what one women won't do the next thot will."

I sat there just looking at the floor thinking, Tan was right. He has been patient enough it was time.

"Yo, is Uncle Troy still leaving for Atlanta today?" I asked Tan breaking the silence in the room.

"Yeah, he left this morning, he will be back Tuesday. Why?" Tan grilled.

"I'm gonna tell my Mama that I am staying at yo house tonight, can you cover for me?" I posed

"You know I got you cuz" Tan answered smiling.

"Let's get dressed when need to hit up Victoria Secret and be back here before 6." I said excitedly jumping up to get myself together.

Tan smiled "Lets hit it!" we both laughed and was dressed and out the door in record time.

CHAPTER 7

I was just tying my sundress over my new lingerie when I heard Ace blow his horn and the car door close. I slipped on my beige 4 inch Christian Louboutin pumps that Ace brought me for Valentine's Day, grabbed my overnight bag and headed for the door. By the time I was up the hall Ace was standing in the kitchen talking to my Mama. They both turned to look at me and smiled.

"You look beautiful baby." my Mama said almost in tears.

"Aww thanks ma." I replied. "I'll call you when I get to Tan's house after we go to dinner." I lied to her Mama with a straight face.

"Ok baby yall have fun!" she kissed me on the cheek and walked out of the kitchen. Ace just stood there staring and grinning like the joker.

"Are those for me?" I asked pointing to the flowers that Ace was holding and seemed to have forgotten about.

"Oh damn! Yes, these are for you. I'm sorry, you just look absolutely amazing." Ace exclaimed handing me the bouquet, grin still plastered on his face.

"Thanks babe, they are beautiful. And you are looking amazing yourself." I said.

"You ready to go?" He asked grabbing my bag and opening the door. We got in the car and backed out of the driveway.

"Where we going?" I probed excited about the evening.

"I got a BIG surprise for you." Ace whispered, "Just sit back and relax."

We drove for about 30 minutes to the outskirts of the city, and pulled into this long driveway that led to this big ass house that looked as if it was in the final stages of construction.

"Where in the hell are we?" I asked looking around. Ace said nothing as he pulled in front of this massive house and parked. Ace got out the car, walked over to my side and opened my door to help me out.

"This house is beautiful. Who lives here?" I questioned again.

Ace remained silent as he grabbed my hand and led me up the stairs to the front door. He put a key in the lock, turned it and opened the door, I was confused. When I walked in the door I was speechless, it was stunning. There were rose petals and candles everywhere, hundreds of them. I walked to the middle of the living room where there was a box sitting on a bed of rose petals. I picked it up and opened the box. In it was a single key. Holding the key in my hand I looked up at Ace again for answers.

"Welcome home baby!" he exclaimed.

"Ace what are u talking?" I asked with attitude, I was almost tired of this guessing game.

He walked over to me explaining "I brought this land about two years ago, right after LilRay and I took over Graham St. I had it for a year before we started dating. Once we became official I started building the house...... for us. I was gonna wait till after graduation to tell you but I couldn't wait any more."

I felt tears fill my eyes and fall down my cheek.

"Don't cry baby." Ace wiped the moisture from my face and grabbed my hand. "Come on let's look at the rest of the house" he said leading me on a tour.

There were beautiful chandeliers, hardwood floors, and marble counter tops, this house had everything you could ever want or imagine in a house.

"There is still some work to be done, just small stuff, but it's mostly finished. And of course, we need to get furniture. It will be ready to move in by graduation" He said as we climbed the stairs leading to the second floor.

The upstairs was simple but nice, 5 guest bedrooms each hosting its own bathroom, a small room for a gym and a library for me. There were a set of double doors that were at the end of the hallway away from the other rooms.

"Is that our room?" I asked.

Ace nodded "I saved the best for last." he whispered in my ear while holding me from behind. "Close your eyes."

"Baby I can't take no more surprises, I might die." I cried.

"Just close your eyes baby." Ace said and I obeyed.

I heard him open the double doors and felt him grab both my hands. He led me into the bedroom, kissed me softly on my lips.

"Ok baby, you can open your eyes." He said finally.

I opened my eyes and looked around, I felt my knees get weak as if I was going to faint. This was the only room that was fully furnished. There was a California King size bed with matching dresser and nightstands, a 60-inch TV mounted on the wall, and a mink throw rug on the floor, the room was the shit. Ace had also placed rose petals and candles all over the room leading from the door to the bed to the master bathroom. In the bathroom, there was a huge Jacuzzi tube, his and her sinks and a large standing shower with multiple shower heads. I looked at Ace and jumped into his arms kissing him.

"So, I guess you like it?' he asked laughing.

"I love it, I love it." I yelled and kissed him again.

"Come on let's blow these candles out so we can go to dinner, I don't want to get you to your uncle house too late." He said.

I smiled and said "How about you go get the food to go we eat here and I stay with you tonight."

Ace looked at me bewildered, "You sure?" he asked.

"Yes baby, I will call the food order in, you go pick it up and I will be waiting for you here. But to tell you the truth I'm really not that hungry." I said trying to sound sexy. Ace was in a state of shock.

"It's whatever you want to do bae. But I have to go get some clothes. I didn't plan on staying here." He said.

"I got you. You know when I go shopping for myself I always shop for you too. I got you 2 outfits, they are in my overnight bag in the car." I responded grinning. Ace could do nothing but laugh.

"Ok babe, I am going to run to the car and get your bag, order us a pizza in case we get hungry later." He said he looked at me and shook his head as he headed outside.

As soon as I heard the front door close I untied my sundress and let it fall to the floor exposing my sexy Victoria Secret red and black bra and panty set. I kept my pumps on as I laid across the enormous bed waiting on him to return. My heart was racing as I heard him come through the door and up the stairs.

"Babe I forgot to ......" he looked up at me and stopped mid-sentence. "Damn!" he let out in a hushed tone.

He walked over to the bed and just stood there staring at me. I raised up on my knees and kissed him.

"Are you sure you want to do this?" he asked "We can wait as long as you need if you not ready."

I looked him in his eyes and said "Baby I am ready, you have proven yourself to me repeatedly, I know I can trust you with my heart and my feelings. I know you will never lie to me. I love you with all my heart. I just ask you to do one thing for me?"

"Anything you ask I got you. What you need baby?" he responded.

I laid back on the bed and said "I just need you to be gentle with me and take your time."

I was so scared but I tried my hardest not to show it. I watched him get undressed down to his Ralph Lauren briefs, before tossing his pants to the floor he pulled out something from his pocket.

"Come here baby." He said to me holding his free hand out. I crawled to the side of the bed where he was standing. He grabbed me by my waist, lifted me and stood me up on the floor. He hugged my tight and whispered in my ear

"I have something for you."

"I don't need nothing else baby this is too much already." I whispered back.

He broke our embrace and held out a small black box in front of me.   "Happy Birthday" he said with a smile and opened the box. In it was another key, but this one was smaller and was attached to a diamond cut link chain. He pulled the chain out and tossed the box to the floor.

"This is the key to my life Jazzell." He said as he placed the key around my neck. "If something was to ever happen to me, if I have to do a long bid or I get killed, this key holds that promise I made to you a year ago."

"What promise baby?" I asked.

"I said that once you were mine I would take care of you for the rest of your life. And I am going to keep that promise in life and death." He answered.

I was so emotional I couldn't do anything but cry.

He kissed me, "Don't cry baby, I told you I got you and I mean it." He said.

"I will never take it off." I said through sobs.

He kissed me on my forehead, then my cheek, then my neck. The kiss on my neck turned into licking. From my neck to the middle of my chest just where my breast met. Ace hands explored my body as he lips made their way to my nipples, sucking and licking them. We moaned at the same time as he kneeled and made a wet trail from my nipples to my stomach before he kissed it. My knees were so weak, I felt I would buckle at any moment. Right before I was about to explode from the inside he stood up, lifted me up and placed me on the bed. He kissed the inside of my thigh, and then he ripped my panties off.

"Were they expensive baby?" He asked as he threw them to the floor.

"Very" I replied giggling.

He laughed and kissed me deeply before burying his face in my wetness. I let out a scream, this was something I'd never felt before. I felt like my skin was on fire. His tongue did a dance with my clit that had my head spinning. I tried to back away because it was so intense but Ace wrapped his arms around my hips so I that couldn't move. I felt as if I was on a roller coaster and we had reached the peak of the highest hill, and then......my back arched without my permission, my body shook uncontrollably and then there was a rush, I could stop it. Ace kissed me and I could taste my juices on his lips and tongue. He wrapped my legs around his waist.

"Hold on to my neck" he whispered. I wrapped my arms around his neck and he lifted, lifting me up with him. He secured my back firmly with one arm and used his free hand to pull the covers back on the bed. He laid me down gently and moved my hair of my face before kissing me again.

"You ok baby?" he asked softly. I nodded and licked my lips. He pulled his briefs and down and off in a fluid motion. Ace rubbed the tip of his dick on my clit and said "Damn bae you so wet."

"Only for you boo" I responded seductively as his dick found its entry point. He gently pushed forward slowly grinding his hips. At first it felt like the greatest thing on earth and then there was a little pain. The further he pushed into me the pain grew. The pain quickly turned into pleasure as Ace pushed his entire dick inside me. The feeling was out of this world as he found his rhythm and helped me find mine. As I let my guard down and we became one, our bodies moved to a beat we shared in our head. That roller coaster feeling came back and before I could gain control my body let loose. Legs shaking, body jerking, pussy gyrating all out of my control.

"I'm bout to cum baby!" Ace exclaimed and started to pump harder and harder before he jumped back, juices shot all over my stomach and titties. He leaned over me breathing hard and panting.

He kissed my forehead and asked "You good baby?" again I nodded as he collapsed on the bed beside me. He laid for a second looking at the ceiling trying to catch his breath. He then rolled off the bed and staggered to the bathroom. I heard water running as I laid in the bed trying to catch my breath as well. Ace came back with a warm washcloth and cleaned up the art he created on my stomach. He threw the washcloth to the floor and hopped in the bed beside me. He wrapped his arms around me, kissed me on my neck and asked again "You ok baby?"

"I'm perfect" I responded. We both drifted off to sleep feeling like we were on a cloud.

I woke up to the smell of food cooking. I looked over beside me and I was alone in the bed. I pulled the covers back and threw my feet over the side, instantly last night replayed in my head and I got goosebumps. I picked my phone up to check the time, 5:06 AM.

"What the fuck is he doing up?" I whispered to myself as I climbed out the bed. I followed the smell of food and made my way to the kitchen.

"Good morning babe, Happy Birthday! I was just about to wake you." Ace said cheerfully as he put eggs on a plate already occupied with pancakes and sliced fruit.

"It's 5 o'clock in the morning, what in the hell are you doing up? And where did you get food?" I asked rubbing my eyes trying to adjust to the light.

"I got up and went for a run around 4AM and there is a Walmart down the streets that's 24 hours. I figured I would make you a birthday breakfast before school." He explained.

"Damn that looks good!" I smiled as he handed me a plate.

When we finished eating Ace looked at his watch and said "We'd better get a move on before we be late."

I reluctantly went upstairs and got dressed.

CHAPTER 8

The school bell was ringing for 1st period as they walked through the doors so Ace didn't have time to walk Jazzy to her class. Instead he kissed her and they both ran in opposite directions mixing with the other students scrambling not to be late. He made it to calculus just before Mr. Rydall was closing the door. As soon as he walked in the first face he saw was Tonya's, glaring at him as if her stare could set him on fire. Ace had forgotten about their run-in at her party until this very moment. He took his seat trying to avoid eye contact but he could feel her eyes burning into the side of his face throughout the entire class. When the bell rang for class to be dismissed Ace was the first one out of his chair. He waited outside the class for Tonya to exit.

"Aye yo Tonya can I holla at you real quick?" he asked when he spotted her walking out with Cheryl.

Tonya smacked her teeth and walked over "What?" she barked full of attitude.

"Look I want to apologize about the other night. I shouldn't have talked to you like that. That was fucked up on my part, I'm sorry." He expressed sincerely.

"You sorry? Why? You trying to butter me up so I don't tell your girl how your tongue was down my throat and your hand was on my ass? Niggas please miss me with that fake ass apology!" She stated rolling her eyes.

"Naw for real I let shit go too far, I am sorry if you felt like I led you on." Ace returned hoping she would accept his apology.

"Led me on? I am a big girl and I ain't pressed for no dick. Please believe if I really wanted yo ass you would be mine. Buts it cool, I'm gonna let you live. I aint gonna tell yo bitch." Tonya declared.

Ace sighed in relief. He dug in his pocket and pulled out three $100 bills, "Buy yourself some lunch, on me, it's my way of apologizing." He smiled at her. Tonya couldn't help but grin, she snatched the money.

"Thanks" she uttered and walked away. "That nigga thinks this shit over, he'd better think again. I got something for dat ass" She said to herself laughing.

Ace was relieved that this shit was over. He walked down the hall smiling, proud that he had handled the situation before it got back to Jazzy.

The first half of my school day was cool, at lunch my Papa had a bouquet of roses and a bunch of balloons delivered to the school. Ace put them in his car so that I didn't have to carry them around all day. Funny thing is a hadn't seen Tan all day, it was weird. Everyone I asked said they hadn't seen her either. I tried to call her but her phone went straight to voice mail, and she hadn't texted me back at all. I was starting to get worried, Tan made a big deal about our birthday week every year, so for her to be missing in action was strange.

"Ace, have you seen Tan?" I asked as he sat down at the lunch table.

"Naw I haven't seen her today; I haven't seen Ray either." He said with a confused look on his face.

"Something is not right; I can feel it." I said getting scared and worried. "I'm bout to call my Papa." I pronounced pulling my cell out.

"You sure you want to do that?" Ace asked "I mean what if they decided to skip school today for whatever reason, do you want to call and dry snitch?" He had a point.

"Well what should I do then?" I probed.

"Nothing, just chill and see what happens." He responded nonchalantly. I wasn't satisfied with that but, but I had no choice but to chill.

"So, what you wanna do today?" I asked Ace changing the subject.

"Just chill, we will see what the rest of the day brings." He said trying not to make eye contact. That was a weird answer, something funny was going on, and Ace was hiding some shit. But I am gonna let this play out. Ace kissed me on the cheek.

"Last night was da shit baby; I been replaying it in my head all day. It was definitely worth the wait" he whispered in my ear.

That gave me goosebumps and made me grin.

I looked at him and said "Yes it was." And kissed him.

I could feel someone staring at me so I did a quick glanced around the crowded cafeteria. There was Tonya sitting in the corner at a table with her crew, she was glaring at us. She didn't even bother to look away when I looked at her, she stared right at me with an evil glare in her eyes.

"Yo what da fuck is that bitch staring at?" I asked not breaking eye contact with her.

"Who?" Ace asked looking in the direction I was staring in.

"That bitch!" I said loud enough that everyone around me could hear. Everyone at our table turned and looked in her direction. She laughed and looked away.

Ace smacked his teeth, "Man let that shit go, it's your birthday. Don't let her ruin it." He said.

"You have saved that bitch on too many occasions, that shit aint gonna play for too much longer!" I roared getting up from the table to throw my trash away before storming out of the cafeteria.

"I'm gonna have to kick that bitch in the throat before the end of the school year." I said to myself as I walked to my locker.

The rest of the day breezed by without incident, 7th period was over before I could bat an eye. I walked out of the class and was surprised that Ace was standing right there by the door.

"My class was dismissed early so I pulled the car up to the front of the," he said as he grabbed the books in my hands.

"Oh ok, well I don't have to go to my locker so I'm ready." I replied. As we made our way to the front of the school I noticed there was a crowd forming outside.

"What the hell is going on." I asked aloud.

"I don't know, let's go see." Ace said with a devilish smile.

We got closer and I could see that everyone was crowded around a red BMW. The closer I got I seen LilRay leaning against it and Tan hanging out the passenger window talking to the crowd of people. LilRay saw me walking up and yelled "HAPPY BIRTHDAY CUZ!" and ran up and gave me a hug.

"Thanks, cuz! What yall got going on? Who car is this? Why yall wasn't in school today?" I had a million questions.

"Damn slow down baby." Ray said laughing, by this time Tan had gotten out of the car.

"Happy Birthday cuz! You like your new whip?" she yelled running toward me.

It was then that I noticed the 2015 Red BMW 550i had a big bow on it. I just stood there in shock, I looked around at Ace, "You knew the whole time?" I yelled playfully punching him in the arm.

He laughed and said "Yeah yo Papa told me about it last week." I snatched the key out of LilRays hand, ran to the driver's side of the car and jumped in. I started the ignition and smiled at Tan as she slipped back in the passenger seat. Ace walked up to the passenger window with 2 brown Chanel boxes, he handed one to Tan and the other to me.

"Happy birthday baby and Happy early birthday Tan." He kissed Tan on the cheek. "Now y'all go joy ride, I will catch up with you later." He said before walking to his car, he hated a lot of attention.

We opened the boxes at the same time and there were the Chanel shades I had been wanting since forever. Mine were black and Tans' was brown, both pair had Chanel written in diamonds on the sides. Simple but classy. I threw my designer shades on my face, threw the car in drive and pulled from in front of the school. I didn't notice Tonya lurking in the background of the crowd.

"That bitch gets on my damn nerves." She said to herself as I left her and the rest of the on lookers in my rearview.

We rode around for a little before headed to my Papa's house. When we pulled up we noticed a Red Infinity QX50 with 30 day tags sitting in the driveway.

"Who car is that?" Tan asked.

"Hell, if I know, let's go in here and be noisy girl." I said laughing.

I parked and as we were exiting the car, my uncle Troy and Papa came out the front door. Both men had the biggest smile on their faces. I ran up to my Papa and hugged him tight.

"Thank you, thank you! I Love it!" I said, burying my face in his chest.

"I'm glad you like it baby. Happy birthday. I am so proud of you." He said kissing me on the forehead. "Thank your cousin, she picked it out."

Tan and I looked at each other and grinned.

"You know I know you like the back of my hand." Tan said smiling proudly, "Now I would have chosen a whip like that one for myself," she said pointing at the Infinity in the driveway.

"Oh, you like that huh?" my Papa said looking at my uncle Troy.

"Yes sir, same color and everything. That thing is sick. Whose car is that anyway?" She asked.

My Papa reached in his pocket and pulled out a set of keys.

"It's yours baby!" he said tossing the keys at her. "Happy Birthday doll!"

"Are you serious?" Tan yell jumping up and down, then hugging him. She ran to the car and hoped in the driver's seat. She started the ignition and rolled down the window

"I'm going for a ride I'll see y'all later!" she yelled.

We all laughed, "That girl crazy" I said to my Uncle and Papa as she backed out of the drive way.

"What's up Cheryl? What you got going on?" Tonya asked after Cheryl answered the phone.

"Shit, bout to head to the mall with my home girl Raelyn. You wanna roll?" Cheryl responded.

"Hell yeah! I got a couple of dollars, I could use the retail therapy. I will meet yall in bout an hour." Tonya answered.

They meet at the food court in Hanes Mall.

"Tonya this is my girl Raelyn she from Cleveland Projects, Tonya this my homie Tonya." Cheryl said introducing the two.

The trio walked through the mall and headed straight for Rainbow. After doing a little shopping they decided to grab some lunch at the food court.

"Damn that bitch got a new whip?" Raelyn said scrolling through her Facebook time line.

"Who?" both Tonya and Cheryl asked at the same time.

"My fake ass cousin Jazzy, her ass sickens me." Raelyn responded with venom in her voice.

"Your cousin? Tonya asked "Big John is your grandfather?" she was confused.

"No Towns is my grandfather, Jazzy's dad was my uncle. But we haven't seen each other since we were little." She responded.

"Oohhhhh Ok." Tonya understood clearly now. "That bitch goes to school wit us, she thinks she da shit." Tonya spat.

Cheryl laughed, "Bitch you just mad cause you been trying to fuck her nigga and he aint giving you no play!"

Tonya shot her a look that could kill, "If I really wanted him I could have him, I'm doing her a favor." She expressed.

"If that's yo fam why you don't like her? I mean y'all blood, right?" she asked Raelyn.

"We fam but she don't act like it. She acts like my grandfather don't exist, especially after my uncle was killed. She thinks Big John is the next thing to Jesus Christ, my grandfather hates his ass." Raelyn explained.

Tonya looked at Raelyn and said "I think I like you! We are gonna be good friends." The girls burst into laughter and continued to eat their lunch.

The next day at school I was standing at Tans' locker waiting on her. It was her birthday and I had a bouquet of yellow roses and a bunch of balloons to surprise her. I was shocked to see her walking down the hall towards me with Tonya and Cheryl laughing and shit like they were best friends.

"Hey cuz!" she bellowed cheerfully as she approached me.

"Happy Birthday cuz!" I responded hugging her and handing her the flowers and balloons. I looked at her two associates and back at Tan. "What's going on?" I asked.

"Nothing just ..." she started to say before loud mouth ass Tonya jumped in

"Damn you got to explain yo'self to her? What she yo Mama?" she said her and Cheryl laughing.

"No bitch I'm yo Mama now stay in a child's place before I whip yo ass!" I shouted. Everyone around us stopped and looked hoping for a fight.

"Hold up yall trippin!" Tan said standing in between us. "Damn Jazzy it's my birthday! Can I have one fuckin day without you making it about you?" she yelled. I was in shock.

"You flippin on me for this bitch?" I asked staring at Tan like she had lost her damn mind.

"Yo I can hang wit who ever I want to. You can't control who I'm friends' wit." She continued while Tonya and her minion snickered. "Look I will holla at you later. Thanks for the flowers and the balloons." She said and walked away with the two girls in tow, leaving me standing there looking stupid. I shook my head in disbelief and walked to my class.

After school I walked to my car to wait on Ace and there the trio was getting into Tans car.

"What the fuck is going on?" I said to myself. I was so engulfed in my disbelief that I didn't notice Ace walk up.

"Hey baby." He said startling me.

"Damn babe you scared me." I said grabbing my chest.

"What's got your mind occupied?" he asked kissing me.

"Tan ass is tripping, she hanging with those birds Tonya and Cheryl." I said almost shouting.

"And?" he asked looking puzzled.

"What you mean and? She knows how those hoes get down, why would she want to rock with them? And then for it to come on suddenly, literally overnight." I exclaimed furiously.

Ace looked at me and said "Babe I understand where you coming from, but you have to let Tan make her own mistakes and decisions."

Deep down Ace was nervous, this couldn't be good, aint no telling what Tonya was telling Tan. But he couldn't show his nervousness in front of Jazzy she would become suspicious. He grabbed me by the waist, "It's still your birthday week, let's go to OUR house and do some more celebrating" he said kissing my ear changing the subject.

That made me smile, "I'm cool with that." I said as he opened the door for me to get into the drivers' seat.

He closed the door and jogged around the car and jumped in the passenger seat.

"Let's go then baby!" he said grinning as I started the car a pulled out of the student parking lot.

"Girl this whip is HOT!" Tonya yelled over Future blaring through the speakers from the back seat of Tans car.

"Thanks girl! My Papa really showed out with this one!" Tan replied turning the music down.

"But damn Jazzy got a BMW, he could have at least got you a damn Benz." Cheryl uttered glancing back at Tonya.

"Naw I'm good, my Papa knows us better than anybody. He knows this is exactly what I wanted." Tan explained.

By this time, they were parked in Tans driveway exiting the car. The girls entered Tans house and immediately Tonya and Cheryl mouths dropped.

"Damn bitch, I don't even feel like I'm in the hood no mo." Tonya said admiring the white leather couches and 70-inch plasma hanging on the wall. Tan laughed feeling proud as she led them to her room. The all removed their shoes and got comfortable as Tan flipped on the TV.

"I'll be right back I'm bout to go grab some snacks and shit." She said as she walked out the door.

As soon as she was out of ear shot Cheryl said, "I told you Tan was cool."

Tonya smacked her teeth and replied, "At the end of the day that's still Jazzy cousin so tread lightly. I don't want to have to fuck that bitch up in her own house."

"I know that shit right!" Cheryl shot back. Tan returned and sat a tray of chips, cookies, and sodas on the floor before turning on her stereo.

"If this was my room I would never fucking leave." Cheryl said kicking back popping open a soda.

"Yeah, it's cool. My dad and Papa makes sure we straight. I can't complain." Tan responded nonchalantly.

"I bet Jazzys' room is the shit too huh?" Tonya asked looking a Cheryl.

"Naw her room is pretty simple. But her closet is a fool. My Papa had extra shelves and shit built in for all her damn bags, shoes and clothes." Tan answered.

"Damn that's what's up." Cheryl retorted. Tonya was getting anxious, she was there for a reason and this shit was taking too long. It was time to go in for the kill.

"So, what's up with Jazzy though? Why she acts like she yo damn mama or something?" she asked Tan.

"Girl she always been like that, she just bossy as hell. I don't see how Ace deal with that shit." Tan said laughing "That nigga scared to do anything." Tonya gave Cheryl a glance.

"He aint that dam scared." Tonya said low but loud enough for Tan to hear.

"What you mean?" Tan asked looking lost.

"Naw I aint trying to start no shit. Let me keep my mouth closed." She responded.

"Start no shit? What, you done heard some shit about Ace?" Tan probed.

"Look you got to promise not to say nothing to yo cousin. I don't want no damn drama. Plus, Ace paid me to keep my mouth closed." Tonya said trying to sound sincere.

"I won't, I put that on my life I aint gonna say shit." Tan promised, waiting on Tonya to spill the tea.

"Well you know Ace and Ray came to my party, right?" Tonya questioned.

"Yeah and?" Tan said.

"Well we were outside sitting on Ray's car sipping on some Cuervo and he got a little touchy feely if you know what I mean." Tonya responded.

"No I don't know what you mean. What happened?" Tan asked.

"Maybe it was just the liquor but he grabbed my ass and kissed me. And tried to get me to take him to my room to fuck." Tonya answered added more to the story.

"Shut the fuck up!" Tan yelled.

"I'm dead ass." Tonya continued, "But you know I wasn't going out like dat. I don't share no dick." Tonya stated.

"Well him and Jazzy gotta fuck first before you can consider that sharing." Tan let slip out before she realized.

"What the fuck you mean? Jaz and Ace aint fucking?" Cheryl asked astonished almost choking on her soda.

Tan knew she had already said to much so she just replied "It aint my business to tell."

"Damn that's why that nigga be on me like do. Well the next week in school, he begged me not to tell Jazzy, he even gave me $300 to keep my mouth shut." Tonya added.

"Bitch you lying!" Tan shouted in disbelief.

"I put that on my Mama." Tonya declared.

"Damn dat shit crazy." Tan said shaking her head.

Tonya looked at her watch "Damn I need to be heading to the house. I gotta get my chores done before my Mama gets off work." Tonya stated standing to leave.

"Ok let me get my keys." Tan said looking around for her purse.

"Naw we good, we will walk, I wanna do a stroll through the hood anyway." She responded slipping on her shoes. Tan walked the girls to the door and they said their goodbyes. Tan was left in a state of shock and confusion, she didn't know what to do, should she tell her cousin about Ace and Tonya? Hell, yeah, she was gonna tell her, fuck Tonya her loyalty lies with her fam. She ran to room, grabbed her cell phone off the night stand and dialed Jazzy's number.

"Hey cuz, what's up?" she answered on the second ring,

"Yo I got something to tell you but you not gonna like it." Tan said.

CHAPTER 9

I was standing at my locker still fuming from what Tan told me last night. I hadn't said anything to Ace yet because I was pissed, I ignored his calls and text all night.

Ace walked up to me, "Hey baby! What's going on wit you? I called you all night and all morning why you aint answering my calls?" he asked.

I looked at him and asked "Is there something you need to tell me?"

He looked terrified. "What are you talking bout Jazzell?" He asked cautiously.

I looked over his shoulder and saw Tonya making her way down the hall, "You sure you don't have nothing to tell me?" I asked again, never taking me eyes of Tonya.

Before he could answer Tonya was walking by us "Hey Ace" she said with a smug grin on her face.

"Aye Tonya can I holla at you for a second?" I said calmly.

"Yeah, what's up?" she responded walking over to us grinning.

"Look I understand you feeling my boo, got this little school girl crush or whatever, but he aint feelin you. So please stop being thirsty." I stated in a condescending tone.

"Thirsty? Bitch please! Aint shit thirsty about me!" she yelled getting riled up, which I knew she would.

"The thirst is real hoe! All these niggas in this school and you all on mine." I taunted.

"Aint nobody checking fo yo nigga bitch, if anything he checkin for me." She exclaimed. By this time a crowd had started forming, Ace just stood there looking stupid not saying anything.

"Bitch please! You better be glad I let him even talk to yo trick ass. Get off his dick, he don't want you!" I cried out.

"Off his dick? Bitch you out yo rabbit ass mind. I guess he didn't tell you what happened at my party?" she said with a knowing smile looking at Ace, the crowd Ohhing, egging us on.

"Yeah bitch he told me he got drunk and lost his mind for a second, just because he kissed you and grabbed that flabby ass doesn't mean shit! He still left yo ass sitting looking stupid and came right to my house where he belongs and told me everything." I bellowed. Both of their mouths dropped.

"Then why the hell did he give me $300 not to tell you if he already did? She asked.

"Bitch prove it! Prove that he gave you some dough, $300 psst that what he gives me for lunch money, get yo life bitch!" I threw back at her, "I am only gonna say this shit one more damn time, Keep yo thirsty ass away from my dick!" I roared.

"Yo dick? That's funny as hell cause from what I hear you don't even know what the dick looks like! You still a virgin, right? No wonder Ace sniffing all up on me!" she laughed and her and Cheryl slapped fives.

I wanted to karate chop that bitch in her throat, but I held my composure. I laughed with them and said,

"You right, yes I'm still a virgin. You throwing the pussy at a nigga and he still don't want you, he aint even smelled mine and he still all on my shit. But you winning though!" I thundered just as the bell was ringing. The crowd roared into laughter. "Next time you even look at him I'm gonna snatch yo spine out'cho asshole! C'mon Ace!" I yelled and proceeded to cut through the crowd to head to my class, Ace right on my heels.

I noticed Tan standing in the back of the crowd, I looked her in her eyes, shook my head and walked away. "Damn, my own fucking cousin." I said to myself because I knew she was the one that told Tonya I was a virgin. I never told her bout the house nor about losing my virginity on my birthday.

"Fuck her too!" I said as I walked in my class and sat down leaving Ace standing in the hall with no kiss goodbye looking confused.

"Babe, what's wrong?" Juice asked Tan as they were sitting in her living room, "You been sulking since I got here, what you not happy to see me?" he asked.

"Naw it's just been a long ass week." She replied. The two had been messing around for months and had went from just seeing each other to dating. Although Tan kept it a secret from her cousins she liked Juice and he seemed to like her. She knew that if she were to tell Lil Ray or Jazzy that Juice is her boyfriend they would flip shit. She couldn't let her Papa find out she was sleeping with the enemy he would be livid.

"Well, are you gonna tell me what happened?" Juice asked pulling Tan closer to him by her waist and wrapping his arm around her.

"Tonya told me about some shit that happened between her and Ace at her party, I told Jazzy and the shit hit the fan the other day in school." She explained. "Now Jazzy is not speaking to me."

"Damn, what the fuck happened? They fucked or something?" Juice probed for more information.

"Naw they kissed and Ace grabbed her ass or some shit." She responded.

"So, Jazzy and Ace broke up?" he asked.

"Shit I don't know. After the blow up in the hall I didn't see Jazzy anymore. It's like she is dodging me." Tan replied sounding mystified. "I called her a few times

but she sent me to voicemail. I know she pissed at me."
She continued.

Now Juice was confused. "Why would she be mad
at you? I mean you did tell her what Tonya told you
right?" he asked with his face screwed up.

"Yeah but I also let it slip that Jazzy and Ace
wasn't fuckin and that she was a virgin." Tan uttered
almost shamefully.

"Damn babe. So, what you gonna do?" he asked.
"Hell if I know." She replied.

"In my honest opinion I said you should just let it
be." Juice declared.

"What you mean?" Tan raised.

"Well I mean you let her know what was up with
her nigga, I mean you kept it a hunnid with her. You
could have easily kept that to yourself. To me that
proves loyalty, if Jazzy can't appreciate that then maybe
yall not as tight as you thought yall was." Juice
explained. "So, what you let a little secret slip? It's not
that serious."

Tan thought about if for a few minutes, "Maybe
you're right." She said.

"I know she family baby, but all she does is boss
you around and treat you like a child. You don't need
her, you got me, I got you babe." He said smiling and
kissing her on the cheek.

Tan smiled "I know baby."

"Besides Jazzy has been in the spotlight way to
long, maybe is time you take over as the princess of the
hood." Juice baited.

"What the hell you talking bout?" she asked
confused.

"I'm trying to be a boss out here, with you as my
girl. I'm gonna take care of you girl, I just need your
help" Juice answered looking Tan in the eyes.

"What you mean? What can I do?" Tan quizzed.

Juice hesitated for a minute the said "Tell me
everything about Big Johns operation."

Tan jumped up "Are you fucking crazy? Have you lost your mind?" she shouted.

"Look your Papa is the only hustler I know that has never been knocked or robbed. I just need to know how he does it, how he moves, you know sorta like a blueprint. That way I can start my own organization and get this money." He explained.

"I don't know Juice. My Papa would kill me if he found out." Tan replied reluctantly shaking her head.

"How would he find out?" he asked. "Look baby" Juice continued "Don't you want me to be able to spoil you? Don't you want to be like Jazzy and Ace? On top running shit. This is the only way."

The thought of her being spoiled with everything she ever wanted ran through her head She smiled as she sat down and rested her head on Juices' shoulder.

"Alright baby I'm with you." She stated, Juice couldn't help but smile as Tan begin to divulge all her family's' business.

"Hello," I said, finally answering the phone after Ace's 100th call this week. It had been a week since the shit hit the fan with Tonya and I will be so glad when it dies down. Hopefully by Monday it will be old news and everyone will be talking and whispering about someone else.

"Bout time you picked up! I've been calling you all damn week." He barked.

"Yo if you gonna yell in my damn ear you may as well hang up now." I yelled back.

"I'm sorry boo, can I please come get you so we can talk?" He begged

"Oooh so now you wanna talk, yo ass should been talkin when you had your tongue down that nasty bitch throat!" I screamed into the phone.

"Look Jazzy please let me come get you, I don't want to talk about this shit over the phone." Ace pleaded.

I thought for a minute before responding "How bout I meet you somewhere? That way if you piss me off more I don't have to ride back in the car with your trifling ass!"

Ace laughed then said "Yo ass is crazy you know that? Ok bet, where u wanna meet?"

I paused contemplating for a minute then I said, "Meet me at home, in an hour." and hung up the phone without another word. I grabbed my purse and my keys and headed out the door, I wanted to talk to my Papa before seeing Ace maybe he can give me some advice on how to handle this shit.

My Papa and I talked for a little while and I headed to meet with Ace. I arrived a few minutes past the hour and was still there before Ace. I backed in and parked facing the house. That night of my birthday replayed in my head and brought a smile to my face. Then it hit me.

"Wait a fuckin minute." I said aloud "That was the night after all that shit went down at Tonya's party!" I went from reminiscing to being pissed off again.

Ace pulled up and parked beside me, I just looked at him in disgust through the glass. He got out the car and walked over to my car door.

"You aint gonna get out?" he asked through the window. I turned my car off and he opened the car door for me to get out. He reached out for a hug and kiss and I turned my head.

"You think you gonna kiss me after you been kissing on that dirty bitch?" I snapped."

Ace smacked his teeth "Come on baby, you trippin. Let's just go in the house and talk." He said grabbing my hand leading me to the front door, of course I followed. He unlocked the door and we walked in. As soon as he closed the door behind us he grabbed me from behind and pulled me close to him. "I'm so sorry baby, I swear didn't nothing happened between me and that girl." He claimed.

I pushed away "How come you didn't tell me then?" I asked looking him square in the eyes.

"I didn't want you to be mad at me." He responded "I was scared you was gonna leave me. Baby she is nothing, she came on to me I was on the liquor I lost my head for a minute" he pleaded.

"But you had every chance to tell me. You brought me to this house and fucked me while lying to me in the process." I screamed starting to get emotional I could feel the tears burning the back of eyes.

"Fucked you? I didn't fuck you, you are my girl, I made love to my woman." He yelled back, "Look" he continued lowering his tone. "I don't want that bitch I am with who I want. I apologize for not keeping it a hunnid wit you. Damn can we get pass this shit and move on?" Ace pleaded.

I looked at him, he looked like he was crushed. "I don't want you speaking to that bitch ever again. If I see you looking at that hoe I will smack fire out yo ass!" I exclaimed.

He busted out laughing, "You know I love it when you talk to me like that." He said as I tried to keep a straight face but I couldn't hold it, I burst into laughter.

"I'm serious nigga! And the next time you give a bitch some money she better be a damn jeweler handing you a big ass ring!" I declared still laughing.

He grabbed me again and pulled me into a deep kiss. While we were kissing, he chuckled again.

"What the hell is so funny?" I asked.

"I like the way you flipped that shit today tho. Tonya raggedy ass thought she was bout to spill some shit." He answered still laughing.

"Oh, you know I wasn't bout to let that bitch have the upper hand." I retorted laughing with him.

He looked me in the eyes and said "I promise it will never happen again. I love you baby; you are the only woman I want for the rest of my life." I kissed him as he and grabbed my hand.

"Come on baby lets go make up for real!" he grinned and said "That's what you need, some good wood. That'll straighten that attitude out." He smacked me on my ass "Get upstairs and take those clothes off!" he directed. I giggled and ran up the stairs while Ace made sure the door was locked before following me. We spent the rest of the weekend in OUR house together, we turned our phones off and secluded ourselves from the rest of the world.

"Damn that bitch Tan didn't waste time, she must have called Jazzy as soon as we walked out the door." Cheryl stated to Tonya.

"I knew she would!" Tonya replied laughing "He paid me not to tell Jazzy Not Tan." Both girls laughed.

"I haven't seen them together all week, you think they gone break up?" Cheryl asked.

"Girl no, that bitch aint gone break up with his ass. But she got something coming for her the way she tried me in the hall like that. That shit been fucking with me all week" Tonya answered.

"What the fuck you plan on doin, I know yo devilish ass. You got some shit up yo sleeve." Cheryl inquired.

"Just wait and see. I aint gonna say shit yet. Ace ass gonna get it too. That reminds me I need yo home girl Raelyn number, text it to me." Tonya demanded.

"Aight I will send it. Aye this my boo beeping in on my other line. I'll hit you later." Cheryl lied before hanging up on Tonya. "That bitch stay with some shit." She said as she texted Raelyn's number to Tonya shaking her head before throwing her phone on her bed.

CHAPTER 10

The next Monday at school it seemed like everyone was watching as Ace and I walked down the hall holding hands.

"Damn all eyes on us." I said to Ace as we approached my locker.

I guess everyone assumed we would break up. I glanced over my shoulder and spotted Cheryl and Tonya standing at Tan's locker with her. We caught eyes for a moment, I just shook my head and turned my attention back to Ace.

"Yo have you seen Lil Ray? I hadn't talked to him since my birthday." I asked.

"Last I seen him was Friday before I came to meet you, but only for a second. He claimed he had some business to handle." Ace replied.

"What kind of business? And why didn't you go with him?" I asked.

"He wouldn't tell me Jazzy. I offered to roll wit him but he said he wanted to go solo. Plus, I was coming to meet you." Ace responded borderline defensive.

I sucked my teeth, "And you haven't heard from him since?" I asked

"Naw I'm gonna text him now and make sure he straight." He said pulling his cell phone from his pocket as the bell rang for 1st period.

"You should've did that last night." I said my voice dripping with attitude, "just let me know if you hear from him." I kissed him on the cheek slammed my locker door and walked off to class.

We were in class for about 30 minutes when I got called to report to the office over the loud speaker.

"What the fuck?" I said to myself as I gathered my things with everyone staring. As I exited the class and walked toward the office I seen Ace walking down the hall with a school administrator and a police officer, he was handcuffed.

I ran up to them, "Baby what's going on?" I asked frantically.

"I don't know. Call my lawyer." he responded.

"Officer what is he being charged with?" I asked the young black officer that was holding on to Ace's arm.

"Ma'am I need you to back up." Was his response as they pushed past me taking Ace through the front door of the school. I watched while they put him in the back of the cop car. I pulled out my cell and quickly called Ace's lawyer. By the time, I as ending the call the principle walked out of the office with a black female officer.

"Miss. Harris this officer needs you to come with her." he stated pointing to the officer. Behind him was Tan being escorted out of the office with yet another officer. I felt as if I was gonna faint.

"What's going on?" I asked.

The female officer responded "I just need you to come down to the station so I can ask you a few questions?" she opened the front door to the school and motioned for me to walk through. They had already placed Tan in the back of the police car when the officer opened the door for me. I was about to slide in the other side but the female officer stopped me.

"Place your hands on the trunk of the car and spread your feet apart." She boomed.

"What?" I said with attitude.

"You heard me." She responded "Place your hands on the back of the car and spread your feet apart."

I did as I was told and she proceeded to search me. She grabbed my cellphone out of my pocket and handed it to the officer that had placed Tan in the car. Through all the commotion I hadn't noticed that the bell had rang dismissing 1st period and half the student body were watching the ordeal through the windows.

"Okay Miss. Harris, have a seat in back please." The officer said.

I slid in the back seat and she slammed the door behind me. Tan and I looked at each other, "What the fuck?" she mouthed at me and I shrugged my shoulders. I looked back at the school doors and my eyes locked on Tonya, standing there with a smirk on her face. I didn't know what was going on but we damn sure getting ready to find out.

We pulled at the police station and were escorted in and down a long ass hallway lined with doors. We stopped at a door marked INTERVIEW ROOM 3.

One officer opened the door and looked at me before barking, "You in here. Have a seat."

I entered the small cold room and the door slammed behind me leaving me alone. There was a metal table in the middle of the room with 3 chairs surrounding it, 2 on one side facing one single chair on the opposite side. I sat in the single chair and waited for what seemed and eternity before two detectives walked in.

"Good morning Miss Harris, I'm Detective Denosia and this is Detective Bennett" a Hispanic man with graying hair stated. Detective Bennett was a very young attractive dark skinned man. Both men sat in the chairs across from me, Denosia placed a folder on the table and opened it. The room was silent as he thumbed through the papers.

"Why am I here?" I asked breaking the silence.

Bennett sat quiet just looking at me with his hands locked resting on the table.

"Miss. Harris, you and your family are in a great deal of trouble, for me to help you you're going have to be completely honest with me." Denosia said.

He turned a picture my way and pointed, "Is this man your grandfather?" he asked.

Before I could answer, Ace's lawyer was bursting through the door.

CHAPTER 11

I woke up to the sun beaming on me through my bedroom window. I reached over and grabbed my cell from the night stand to check the time, 8:29AM. I rolled over and stared at the ceiling, waiting for a sign telling me that it was all a bad dream, a horrible nightmare. My phone chimed in my hand causing me to jump. My alarm clock sounded letting me know it was indeed real and time for me to get my ass up.

I still hadn't gotten used to Ace not being the first voice I hear in the mornings. I threw the covers back, climbed out of bed and headed to the shower. As the hot water ran down my slumped back that horrid day flashed in my head as it did all day every day, I still couldn't wrap my head around what the fuck happened. My thoughts were interrupted by banging on the bathroom door.

"Hurry up Jaz! We're going to be late" A voice boomed from the opposite side of the door.

"I'm coming damn, I just got in!" I yelled back. I hastily washed and rinsed my body and turned the water off. I wrapped myself in a towel and exited the bathroom with attitude, stomping through my room. Tan was sitting on the edge of my bed fully dressed with her legs crossed and arms folded.

"Damn what the fuck you rushing me for? We don't have to be there till 11." I barked.

"You know yo ass slow as hell." Tan replied. She looked around the massive bedroom. "I still can't believe Ace had this big ass crib built for you. She said looking around "I was wondering what the hell he was doing with all his money."

I just looked at her, rolled my eyes and continued to get dressed. There was a knock at the door and Cyn poked her head in.

"We still going to see Mama and grandma?" she asked.

"Yes, we're leaving in bout 15 min. I'm almost ready" I responded.

After I was dressed Tan, Cyn, Kia and I piled in my car and drove the 35 minutes to the county jail. This has been our ritual every Saturday. Just Tan and I went alone on Wednesday mornings and I went alone on Thursdays.

3 months ago, my whole world was turned upside down. While I was at school the Forsyth County Police Dept were gearing up to tear my world apart. They simultaneously ran up in my grandparents' house, my uncle Troy house, my aunt Tissie's house as well as my home. They arrested everyone in my family including my grandmother as well as every single member of my Papa's organization. The only one that hadn't been arrested and is still missing in action was Lil Ray.

They searched and seized every business that Big John owned as well as all his properties. The only thing we had left was my mom's hair salon, being that was purchased with the money from my father's insurance and the cars my Papa purchased for Tan and I because they were purchased in Tan's mother's name. Unfortunately, with my mom, aunts and grandma were locked up there was no one to run the salon. I tried to hold on to it as long as I could but I eventually had to sell it. The feds froze all the bank accounts and took every dollar out of the safes into evidence. My sisters, Tan and I were forced out of our homes and had to move into the only place that no one knew about, the house Ace built for us. Being that's the land nor the house were in Ace's name, the feds could not touch it.

My Papa and uncles were being held on one side of the county jail while my grandma, Mama and aunts were on the opposite side. On Saturday mornings Tan and I would take my sisters to see my Mama and grandma. Then we would cross the street and visit my Papa and uncles that afternoon. On Wednesdays Tan and I visited my aunts and every Thursday I tried to see

Ace but for some reason my visit kept being denied and not receiving a single phone call since he had been locked up was making matters worse.

I feel like I have the weight of the world on my shoulders. I am taking care of my sisters, handling the lawyers, and trying to hold my family down all by myself. Tan don't really give a fuck about nothing but herself, Juice went missing and stopped answering her calls right after all that shit went down with my family and Tan has been hoeing ever since, fucking with any nigga that paid her any attention. I did manage to still graduate, but do to circumstances neither Ace nor I walked across the stage with our peers. Instead our diplomas were mailed to us.

Along with the salon, I sold almost everything I owned to put a little bit of furniture in the house, and pay the utilities up for a few months. Now the only thing I own is my car, the house, a few clothes and shoes, and the necklace Ace had given me on my birthday which I never took off.

We arrived at the jail at exactly 11 AM, signed in and were seated at a table while we awaited my Mama and grandma to be released for their visit. The guards escorted the women into the visiting room about 10 minutes later. My grandma and Mama came in both smiling and happy to see us. We exchanged hugs and everyone sat down. It was normal chit chat for most of the visit the when it was almost over my Mama sent my sisters to the other side of the room to get a snack out of the vending machine.

"Have you heard anything from the lawyers?" Mama asked me once my sisters were out of ear shot.

"Nothing yet, they said they would only contact me when they have news." I responded trying to sound hopeful. "How are you holding up?" I asked.

"We're good. You know we aint got no worries in here. Your Papa made sure of that." Grandma said with half a smile. The twinkle in her eye was completely gone. I could tell she was putting up a brave front for Tan and me.

"I am worried about you and the girls" my Mama stated. "What are you doing for money? Where in the hell is yo cousin?" she asked.

"Mama I have looked everywhere, I have asked around no one has seen nor heard from Lil Ray. His phone was going straight to voicemail at first now it's disconnected." I explained. "I have sold everything that I can sell. I am running out of money. I have to figure something out. We have to survive at least till yall come home."

"Look, you know what you gotta do baby. You have to take care of your sisters and your cousin." Mama stated.

"I don't need nobody to take of me! I can take care of myself!" Tan exclaimed almost yelling. Up until this point she had been quiet. "Everybody act like Jazzy is so grown and I'm a child or something. Yall keep forgetting we the same age."

My grandma and Mama looked at her as if she had two heads.

"Who are you talking to in that tone?" my grandma asked. "Don't let this orange jumpsuit fool you! I will still beat yo ass in here and not one of this guards would bat an eye!"

Tan just sat there sulking like a 2-year-old not saying a word the rest of the visit.

We didn't stay long because I had to get across the street to see my Papa. Tan had an attitude by this time so she decided to take Kia and Cyn to get something to eat instead of going to see him.

I signed in, was searched, and was seated at a table in no time. My Papa walked in smiling, even in an orange jumpsuit and shackles he is still the most handsome man I ever seen in my life.

"Hey baby" he greeted as he walked as fast as he could with shackles on his feet.

"Hey Papa!" I exclaimed standing up to hug him "Where is uncle Troy?" I asked looking behind him.

"I asked him to sit this visit out. I wanted to talk to you about something" he replied "where is your cousin and your sisters?" he quizzed as we sat down.

"I sent them for food. Tan got an attitude and I didn't want her to bring that negative energy in here." I answered.

"Good!" he responded "That makes it easier for me to talk to you with no interruptions."

"What's going on Papa?" I asked.

"I finally got my indictment papers and copies of the search warrants yesterday. And I am confused as hell baby girl." He stated.

"Why? What did they say?" I asked starting to feel nervous

"There was no mention of any drugs taken into evidence in the paperwork. And neither Ace nor Lil Ray's name is on ANY of the warrants or indictments."

"WHAT?" I exclaimed almost yelling "What are you saying? What do you mean?"

"We had a bail hearing and the judge denied bail for all of us, saying that we are a flight risk." He informed. "They have to have something on me to keep holding us like this with no bond.

I stat her flabbergasted not knowing what to say.

"I don't know what to think right now. I am waiting for my Discovery Packet from me lawyer so that I can get a clear understanding of what is up. Have you spoke to Ace?" he asked staring me in my eyes.

"No, I have been trying to visit him every week but my visits keep being denied." I explained.

"Look I didn't want to say nothing before but Ace aint in here, I have asked around and he is not in the jail, you sure he got arrested?"

"Yes Papa I'm sure. I saw them put him the back of the cop car in cuffs." I explained thinking back to that dreadful day at school.

"Jazzell every one of my soldiers has been accounted for except for them two. ALL OF THEM!" he looked as though he wanted to cry.

"Papa I'm not understanding. This can't be right." I felt as I was going to faint.

"Baby girl listen to me. I know you got a lot on your shoulders but you are gonna have to hold this family down till I can figure out a way to beat this shit." He said lowering his voice to a hushed tone. He looked around before leaning in closer to me before saying "You gonna have to take over and run the business."

I sat there quiet for a few moments trying to think of a response but my mind was blank.

"Jazzy, my connect is gonna call you and he gonna make sure you straight. All you have to do is get you a few soldiers and you good." He explained like it was just that simple.

"Papa I don't know. I mean we hot right now." I stated.

"Baby I have taught you everything you need to know. You got this!" He avowed in a serious tone.

Before I could say anything, a buzzing sound rang out letting us know that visiting hour was over.

"I love you baby girl, I am depending on you. Be waiting for that phone call." He said as he stood to walk away.

Everyone around me was saying goodbye to their loved ones and heading towards the exit. I just sat there in a daze not know what my next move was gonna be. I finally snapped out of it and made my exit toward the car where Tan and the girls were waiting on me. I was silent the whole ride home. My Papa was right, it's time for me to boss up. I got a family to feed.

After I dropped my cousin and my sisters off I decided to ride by Ace's apartment. His car was parked outside, but I could tell by the amount of dirt on it that it hadn't been moved in a while. I had the key to his place, so I let myself in. I looked around for some sort of clue or sign but there was nothing. Everything looked dusty and untouched as if no one had been here for months. It's like this nigga disappeared into thin air. It made no sense to me.

CHAPTER 12

I woke up to my phone ringing nonstop. I picked up the phone and looked at the caller ID, I didn't recognize the number so I hit ignore, tossed the phone on the bed and rolled over. It rang again and I instantly caught an attitude. "Who the hell is calling me this early?" I asked myself as I picked up my phone.

"Hello" I answered, my voice dripping with venom.

"Jazzell?" a man said with a Spanish accent.

"Who is this?" I asked still half sleep.

"Angelo" he replied. The sound of his name made me sit straight up. I was wide awake now. I have heard my Papa speak of him almost my whole life but I had never seen him or until today never heard his voice.

"Good morning Mr. Angelo. I'm sorry I didn't answer when you called I didn't recognize the number." I explained throwing my covers back and hoping out of bed. I don't know why I was so nervous, I had started pacing the floor.

Angelo chuckled "No no Senorita, no Mr. just Angelo." He said.

"I'm sorry Mr..... I mean Angelo." I responded.

"Are you available to meet today.... Say noon?" he asked.

"Of course," I retorted glancing at the clock on my nightstand "Where?" was my next question.

"Your home." He replied.

"Ok I will send you the address." I answered.

"No need I know it." He returned. "See you soon." He stated before disconnecting the call. I exhaled the breath I had been holding thru the entire conversation.

The doorbell rang as I was in the kitchen washing dishes and it startled me. I looked at the clock on the microwave before heading to the door, it read 11:59. My palms were sweating and my heart rate was on a million when I finally reached the door.

"Who is it?" I asked looking through the peephole.

"It's Angelo" He responded. I could only see the back of his head, I waited a few seconds to see if he would turn around but he didn't. Finally, I took a deep breath and opened the door. I was greeted by a handsome Hispanic gentleman with a wide smile. I could do nothing but stare as he was the sexiest man I had seen in my life.

"Hola Senorita...... Peudro entrar?" he asked.

"Excuse me?" I responded with a confused look.

"May I come in?" he repeated in English chuckling.

"Oh of course." I responded stepping to the side for him to enter the house.

"My apologies I don't speak Spanish." I said a little embarrassed.

"Oh, it's quite alright, I was just messing around." He said as I closed and locked the door. When I turned to face him he was staring at me.

"My my you have grown into such a beautiful young lady." He stated looking me admiring me from head to toe. "How are you?" he asked looking me directly in my eyes.

"I'm ok giving the circumstances." Was my response with a half a smile.

His gaze dropped to my neck, he reached up and gently touched my necklace, "That is an interesting charm for a necklace ... A key......A gift from someone special? does it belong to anything of importance?" he asked.

"To be honest I am not sure what it opens or if it opens anything for that matter. Yes, it was a gift from a good friend." I responded.

"Interesting" he responded breaking his gazing and looking around the massive living room "You have a beautiful home Senorita. Ace did really well." He said as he begins to walk toward the kitchen.

"Thank you. I didn't realize that you knew Ace" I responded in a puzzled tone.

Angelo stopped in his tracks turned and faced me. "Maybe that's a good thing." He responded.

I was confused, "What do you mean?" I asked.

"I will explain later." He threw at me. "Tan is out and your sisters are home, yes?" he asked glancing at the stairs.

"Correct, Tan is not home but my sisters are upstairs in their room." I answered. He was making me uneasy with all the questions that he already seemed to know the answers to.

"Very well then, shall we discuss business Jazzell?" Angelo asked rubbing his hands together.

"Of course, and please call me Jazzy." I answered.

"I prefer Jazzell, such a classy name for a classy young woman." He retorted smiling. He had a smile that would make your knees buckle.

"Ok" was my response. "Shall we talk in the sitting room?"

"That would perfect." He said gesturing for me to lead the way.

We sat a talked for hours. We discussed everything from how much product he would give me a week to how it would be delivered. He also assured me that he would send a few guys to help me move the product and some for security. He helped my come up with the perfect way to run my organization to remain under the radar. The more we talk the more comfortable I got with him, by the end of our conversation I felt like Griselda Blanco ready to build my drug empire. Unbeknownst to us there was someone listening to our entire conversation.

Before he left he went to his car and got an eight ball of coke. "I'm only gonna show you this one time." He said.

"But why do I need to learn how to cook it, aint that what my soldiers are for?" I asked confused.

"Jazzell, you have to start from the bottom, you need to know everything about the business to run a successful organization." He explained.

Angelo showed me everything I needed to know before cleaning the kitchen and finally preparing to leave. As I was walking him to the door I asked. "Can I ask you a question?"

"Sure" he responded

"How did you know where I lived? No one knows about this place." I quizzed.

"You will quickly learn that I know everything. So be sure to always tell me the truth. I know the truth before you even think about the lie to let it come out your mouth. And I have been watching Ace for some time now. It was always something about him that didn't sit well with me." Angelo declared.

I just shrugged my shoulders and kept quiet, I didn't know what to say or think about Ace at this point. There are so many unanswered questions.

He reached out to hug me and kissed me on both checks, "Adios Hermosa. You will be hearing from me soon." He said and left.

Once Angelo was gone I just sat in the living on the couch staring out the window. My life was getting ready to change and I had no choice but to be ready.

CHAPTER 13

A week had gone by and I heard nothing. I woke up early Thursday morning and wet to visit my Aunt Tissie, being that Ray was MIA I wanted to make sure she was good. When I returned home there was a small box on my porch. I rushed in the house and tore open the package addressed to me. It was a prepaid cell phone. I powered it up and 2 seconds later it rang.

"Hello" I answered apprehensively.

"Senorita Jazzell." Angelo's voice rang from the other end.

"Good afternoon." I responded happy it was him. I had not been able to stop thinking about him since our first encounter.

"Meet me at the 10th street diner downtown Thomasville." He demanded "1 hour." He said before hanging up the phone.

I ran upstairs and changed from the sweat pants I was wearing to some jeans and an off the shoulder shirt and headed out the door. Thomasville was about a 25-minute ride from and I didn't want to be late.

I arrived 15 minutes early and backed into and parking space facing the building. I expected to be waiting on Angelo when he arrived but to my surprised he was sitting in the last booth in the corner waiting on me. He stood as I walked toward him and reached out to give me a hug.

"Hola Senorita." He said smiling kissing me on my cheek.

"Hola Senor Angelo." I responded before sliding into the booth.

"Estas en hungaria?" he asked.

"No sir I'm fine I ate before I came." I responded.

He looked a little surprised. "Hablas espanol ahora?" he asked chuckling

"Muy poco." I responded "I have been doing a little studying over the past week." I explained.

"I can say that I am impressed." He stated smiling.

I couldn't help but blush a little bit.

"My associate will be delivering the product to you this evening. He will prepare and package it for you and distribute it amongst a few of my guys. This is the only time this will happen this way. So, pay attention because next time you will be doing it yourself. I will contact you at the end of the week to collect my money. I will call the phone I called you on today with a meeting spot."

"Ok" was all I could say.

"You will receive a new throw away phone every two weeks. It is very important that you discard the old phone once you receive the new one." He continued.

"I understand." I responded.

We sat and talked for a few more minutes before I dismissed myself to leave. Before I walked away from the table Angelo said "By the way, you look very nice today."

A smile spread across my face and I felt butterflies in my stomach. I know I shouldn't be crushing on my Papa connect but it was something about him that had me intrigued.

By 6:30 I was back home, in my sweatpants, laying across my bed tripping off Snapchat when my doorbell rang. I ran downstairs to the door and looked thru the peep hole. It was a tall dark skin man with long dreds. I asked "who is it?" thru the door.

"Santiago." He responded "Angelo sent me."

I opened the door and there stood a piece of heaven right on my doorstep. "damn the whole squad is sexy" I thought to myself.

"What's up Jazzell." He said as he walked thru the door. The smell of his cologne lingered at my nose.

"My boys will be calling in a few so we don't have much time. You ready to go?" not even making eye contact with me.

"To go where?" I asked "What you talking bout?"

"To the spot." He stated "You didn't expect me to cook all that shit up here did you?" he asked looking at me like I was crazy.

"Oh ok…. Well let me change my clothes." I responded feeling stupid.

"Yo you got something to drink?" he asked headed for the kitchen as I headed for the stairs.

"Look in the fridge it should be something in there." I responded.

"No I mean DRINK DRINK …. like some Hennessey or something." He exclaimed.

"Naw I'm sorry. I don't drink like that. Not old enough to buy liquor homie." I shrugged before jogging up the stairs to my room to jump in the shower. I washed as quick as I could and wrapped up in a towel.

"Now what am I going to wear?" I asked myself standing in the middle of my closet.

There was a knock then Tan burst through my bedroom door. "Yo who the hell is that downstairs?" she asked. "He fine as hell." She yelled, being loud on purpose.

"Close the damn door and lower your voice." I whispered loudly.

She closed the door and plopped on my bed. "Yo that's you? you going on a date?" she asked sounding shocked.

"Naw that my connects people. We just going out to talk some business that's all. And get your ass of my bed with your street clothes on!" I responded.

She smacked her teeth "Yo connect? What the hell you talkin bout?" she probed getting off the bed and taking a seat at my vanity.

"I'll tell you bout it later." I said waving her off.

She just shrugged "Whatever... Damn bitch, he sexy!" she exclaimed.

I rolled my eyes and continued to scan my closet. I finally decided on a pair of light blue ripped jeans and sheer red long sleeve shirt. I proceed to lotion my body and get dressed while Tan played around with my makeup running her mouth about god knows what, I wasn't really paying her any attention. After I was dressed I unwrapped my hair, drowned myself in Pure Seduction by Victoria Secret, slipped on my blue and red Farragamo pumps and headed downstairs with my cousin right at my heels.

As soon as I hit the bottom step Santiago stood up from the couch. "Damn" he said staring at me.

I blushed and there was an awkward silence.

"Ummm, so where yall headed?" Tan asked being noisy. "And what time should I expect yall back?"

"Excuse me?" I asked looking at her like she had lost her mind. "Girl bye.... I'll be back when I get back." I declared and rolled my eyes at her.

I looked at Santiago "You ready?" I asked

"Yeah let's hit it!" he exclaimed a little too excited.

We left Tan standing in the middle of the living room floor and headed out the door. Even though that's fam I still don't rock with her like that after that whole Ace and Tonya shit.

Santiago open the passenger side door for me to slide into his black on black Dodge Charger.

"You have a nice whip." I said as he climbed in to the driver's seat.

"Thank you. Your shit is hot too! But I'm a Mercedes man myself." He retorted.

We rode with little talk, only John Legend playing through the speakers. I was quite surprised that he was listening to R&B, I figured he would have Gucci or Jezzy blasting the whole time.

When we arrived to our destination he hurriedly jogged over to myside to open the door and help me out of the car. I looked around and was immediately uncomfortable. I don't really venture outside of my hood to often and if I did it certainly didn't fuck around in no damn Boston Projects, this is my dad's old hood.

I kept my mouth closed as Santiago popped the truck and grabbed two bookbags out.

"Come on." he said as he leads the way to the building ahead of us.

He knocked on the door and a few seconds later someone came and peeked through the window before opening it.

Santiago walked in with me trailing close behind him. As soon as we stepped into the kitchen the two young boys that where occupying the raggedy apartment stood up and left without saying a word.

Santiago looked at his watch "Shit Its almost 8.... we need to get this shit poppin. Have a seat." He demanded pointing to a fold out card table and chair "set" that stood in the middle of the kitchen.

He took the book bag off his shoulders and proceeded to empty its contents. I watched as he laid 6 bricks of cocaine on my kitchen counter and busted them open.

"Pay attention." He said

I watched his every move while sitting there in silence. He moved so quick as if this was all he was born to do. In no time the shit was cooked up and ready for packaging.

He looked at me with his dark piercing eyes. "Now I need you to pay close attention.... matter of fact come here and help me." He said waving me over.

I stood and walked over to him and he handed me a razor blade. He took a second scale out of his bag and begin to show me how to cut, weigh and bag the drugs. It took me no time to catch on and before I knew it we had established a rhythm without a word being spoken.

"So, you are Angelo's new protégé?" He asked breaking the silence.

"Protégé"? …. Naw I am just trying to maintain till my Papa comes home. Angelo is helping me, that's all." I explained.

"Your Papa?" he asked puzzled.

"Yeah Big John." I responded.

"Oh shit! You're Big Johns granddaughter! It all makes sense now." He exclaimed.

"What you mean? What makes sense?" I quizzed, stopping what I was doing and looking at him.

"Angelo looks to your Papa like an uncle, even though he was Big Johns connect. He got mad respect for him, he is a good dude though. Now I understand why he sent me to show you what's up……Angelo usually doesn't do shit like this." He explained.

I smiled and continued what I was doing.

"But he didn't tell me you were this fine!" he stated grinning, grilling me from head to toe.

"You even look good in sweat pants." He responded still grilling me. "You aint got a nigga?" he asked.

"I don't know" was my response my voice dropping low. Ace face popped into my head and I was snatched back into reality quick.

"What you mean you don't know?" He asked with a puzzled look on his face.

Before I could answer there was a loud knock at the door.

He exited the kitchen leaving me alone with my thoughts.

"What up fam" I heard him say as he greeted whoever was responsible for that loud ass knock. "We almost done. Come on help us finish."

He returned to the kitchen followed by a tall, lanky light skinned dude with a short cut.

"Jazzell his is my nigga Biggs, Biggs this Jazzell." He introduced us.

"I know Jazzy." Biggs said. "You Ace peoples, right?" he asked.

Santiago looked at me with a shocked look on his face.

"Something like that." I answered trying to avoid eye contact with them both.

"Nice to finally meet you though." Biggs said, then there was an awkward silence.

"Yo so where the rest of the crew at?" Santiago asked Biggs.

"Angelo told me to come dolo....... Now I see why." He stated looking my way.

Santiago laughed "Exactly." He said "But anyway let's get this shit done so we can get the fuck up out of here."

We finished while having small chit chat and Biggs was out the door wit the dope not long after he got there. Santiago and I were in the car leaving shortly after.

He looked at his watch again "Damn it's still kinda early ... Lets go out to get some drinks."

I looked at him like he was crazy. "Didn't you hear what I said? I'm only 18 dude." I stated speaking louder.

"Yo don't worry bout all that.... I got you." he declared.

"I don't know.... I mean I don't know you like that." I said hesitantly.

"If I wanted to do something to you it would be done already." He said matter of factly as he headed for downtown Winston.

Bout 10 minutes later we were pulling in a small parking lot to what looked like an old warehouse, there was no signs on the building and there were only a few cars in the parking lot. Santiago parked got out and walked around to my side to open my door.

"Oh lord! Where you got me?" I asked as we made our way to the entrance.

"Just chill .... you good I promise" he said opening the door for me.

I walked in and was immediately blown away. The outside of the place did the spot no justice. I felt like I wasn't even in Winston no more. The decor was beautiful and fresh. There weren't many people in there but you could tell everybody was on their grown and sexy date night type shit.

"Good evening Mr. Jamison. Would you be sitting at the bar or would you like your usually table." The hosted greeted us as we walked through the door. She looking at me with a strange look as if she was shocked to see me or something. She looked familiar to me but I could not place where I knew her from.

"Hey Raelyn. My usually table is fine thanks." He responded.

"Perfect. Will you and your date be needing menus?" she asked.

"Yes, we will be having dinner." He responded.

"Ok, right this way." She said never taking her eyes off me as she grabbed 2 menus and walked toward the dining room area.

We followed her to a secluded table in the corner by the window. Santiago pulled my chair out as the hostess placed the menus on the table.

"Enjoy your meal." She said with a twinge of attitude before rolling her eyes and walking away.

"What's that all about?" I asked as Santiago took his seat across from me.

"Hell if I know, I come here all the time, she has never acted like that." He explained

"Maybe she got a little crush on you." I said laughing.

"Naw because I have brought plenty of chicks in here, and she was cool. Maybe it's you." he responded raising his eyebrow.

"She does look familiar, but I can't place where I know here from." I responded looking over at her.

"Well anyway. What you want to drink?" he asked looking at the menu.

"Hell, I don't know.... I told you I am not much of a drinker. You order for me." I responded smiling at him.

"You know that smile of yours is deadly." He said grinning at me.

I acted like I didn't hear him "This is a nice spot." I said looking around. "How long has it been here?"

"Bout 3 years. My OG from my hood owns it, it's my little duck off. Few people know about it and you have to be a member to come in." he explained.

"That's what's up" I said just as the waitress walked up to our table.

"Good evening, can I start you guys off with something drink?" she asked.

"Yeah I would like my usually and a glass of Pinot Grigio for the lady." Santiago said taking charge.

"Perfect, are you ordering food as well?" she asked.

"Yeah again I would like my usual and the salmon platter for her." He stated again.

"Cool I will put that in and be right back with your drinks." She said and hurried away from the table.

We sat and talked for a few minutes. When our drinks arrived, I excused myself to the bathroom to wash my hands before our food came. As I was headed back to our table I felt like someone was watching me. I did a quick glance around and didn't notice anything weird so I proceeded to my seat. As I got closer to the table I noticed that there was a man seated in my seat, his back was turned to me so I couldn't see his face. Santiago stood just as I reached the table and reached out to grab my hand.

"I would like you to meet my OG." Santiago said.

The gentleman stood and turned, when finally seen his face I could have died right where I was standing at.

"Jazzell" he said looking as shocked as I was feeling.

I straighten up and regained my composure. "Hello Towns." Was my response.

He pulled the chair out. "Please have a seat." He said motioning for me to sit down.

I just wanted to get the hell up out of there. But I sat instead.

Santiago looked confused. "How do you know each other?" He asked looking at the both of us.

"I will let Jazzell explain that to you. Enjoy your meal." Towns said and prepared to walk away. He stopped suddenly and turned.

"It is really nice to see you." he said "I'm so sorry to hear about your Grandfather. I pray that he is well." He finished before walking away.

I didn't want to look at Santiago so I just stared at the table, not even noticing my food was sitting right in front of me.

"So......what's up?" Santiago poked. "How do you know Towns?"

"He is my grandfather." I responded softly.

"Your grandfather? How?" he asked in a hushed tone like it was a big secret he didn't want anyone to hear.

"My father was his son." I explained "He was killed some years back."

"Damn, I have known that man my whole life. He taught me everything I know about the game. How come I never seen you around?" he asked.

"I was raised by my Mamas' side; Big John is my Mamas' dad. I never really rocked with my dad's people like that." I explained.

"Well that explains why the hostess was acting like that, that's Towns granddaughter, shit your damn cousin, Raelyn." He said laughing "You don't even recognize yo own people."

"Like I said, I don't rock with that side like that." I said with a slight attitude.

Before he could ask me any more questions the throw away phone started ringing loudly in my purse. I hurriedly fumbled through my purse and pulled it out.

"Hello" I said hastily catching the call right in time before it ended.

"Good evening Senorita Jazzell." Angelo's voice sounded like music coming through the phone.

"Good evening Senor Angelo." I replied looking at Santiago.

"I have a shipment coming tonight and need you to go pick it up." He said getting right to the nature of his call.

"Ok...." Was all I could say.

"Santiago knows all the details." Angelo stated before disconnecting the call.

I threw the phone back in my Purse and looked at Santiago as he received a texted message.

"I guess we headed to Mt. Airy." He said without looking at me.

We ate quickly, he paid the bill and we headed out the door. I was about to make my way to the passenger seat when Santiago said "Naw you drive." And threw the keys in the air.

"But I don't know where we going." I said catching the keys before they hit the ground.

"You know how to get to Mt. Airy don't you?" he asked.

"Yeah." I replied.

"Just get us there and I got you" he said as he climbed in the passenger seat.

I started the car but before heading out the parking lot I paused "Hold up...How did he know we were together?" I asked.

Santiago laughed "Trust me...he knows everything."

We laughed and sped toward 52 North.

We were on the highway halfway to Mt. Airy riding in silence, vibing to J. Cole and I could feel Santiago looking at me like he wanted to say something.

"WHAT?" I asked finally turning down the music.

"Nothing man, forget it. "he said shaking his head.

"Naw what's up? What is it?" I asked.

"So, you used to fuck wit that nigga Ace huh?" he asked.

"No I didn't used to fuck with Ace that was my nigga. We were in a relationship." I said.

"So, what happened?" He asked.

"Damn noisy!" I responded.

"Naw for real, why yall break up?" he asked in a serious tone. "A nigga like me would have never let something like you go."

I sat there quiet for a minute acting if I was concentrating on the road. Then a finally responded, "He used to work for my Papa, when my Papa got locked up so did Ace and I hadn't heard from him since. I tried to visit him but my visits kept getting denied. It's like he disappeared."

"Damn" he responded "I have known Ace for a little minute. His Mama used to work for Towns before she started getting high. That's how I meet him. he was a cool man though."

"So, since you all in my business let ask you something. How did you end up working for Angelo instead of Towns since you look up to him so much?" I probed.

"I fucks with Towns but I don't like the way he handles his workers. He treats them like shit and I aint wit that. I meet Angelo through this Dominican chick I used to fuck wit. Her and her home girls used to bring shit across the border for him, she introduced us and he put me on." He explained.

"Oh, so what happened to her?" I asked.

He looked me dead in my eyes and said "Angelo had her killed."

My heart dropped into my stomach. "Why?" I asked.

"He found out she was planning on having him robbed, so he merked her off." He responded.

"That shit don't bother you?" I asked.

"She was the one moving funny. That's what happens when you living foul." He shrugged his shoulders, "Besides me and her wasn't like that we just fucking and getting money together, nothing serious."

"Oh" was all I could say.

We didn't say to much more the rest of the ride. We go to our destination, picked up the shit and was back on the highway in no time.

"Where we going?" I asked halfway back to Winston.

"To your crib." He responded. "I'm dropping you off and I'm going home I'm tired as hell."

When we got to my driveway he jumped out and walked me to the door.

"Yo I'm gonna hit you tomorrow we have to make some rounds, introduce you to the crew so they will know who you are. At this point I would be surprised if half of them already knows you" He announced.

"Whatever...I can't help that I am well known" I responded unlocking my door and stepping into my doorway.

"That could be a gift and a curse baby girl." He said and proceeded to walk down the front stars. "I will check you tomorrow, good night." he threw at me over his shoulder as he walked to his car.

I closed and locked the door, went upstairs, and went straight to bed.

The next day Santiago was there bright and early, after we made our rounds we ended up spending the whole day together. Day after day, week after week we were together every day, getting money and enjoying each other's company. We had the best product in the city and everybody in the squad was eating. Towns and his crew had shit locked down on the north and west side and we owned the east and south side. We respected each other's boundaries and there were no problems. Angelo always got his money on time and it was never a cent short. I could pay the lawyers' fees, keep money on my peoples' books and keep my sisters living in the lifestyle they were accustomed to. Tan even stepped up and I put her on and she was doing the damn thing bringing in more money than any of my other soldiers. Our bond had gotten back to where it was before and we had gotten back tight again. Life was good again.

CHAPTER 14

One night Santiago and I were in my room counting money getting it prepared to drop to Angelo the next morning. We had gotten a bottle of Hennessey and had been sipping all night so by the time the money was counted and the bottle was gone we were both drunk as fuck.

"Yo Angelo gonna flip shit when he gets this. We have never seen numbers like these from our block.!" He said closing the brief case and sliding it under my bed.

"Yeah the crew did good this week. Tan brought in over $10k by herself." I responded proud of my cousin.

"Yo lets watch a movie." Santiago said getting up from the spot in the floor he was sitting in and stretching across my bed.

"Yo ass gonna be sleep before the movie even start" I said doing the same. "And I done told yo ass if you are gonna lay across my bed you need to take those dirty ass clothes off!"

"Oh, you want me to take my clothes off?" he sang seductively raising up to kneel on the bed.

"Yes, I don't like street clothes on my bed, you done been all outside and shit." I said flipping through movies on my Amazon Fire Stick to find something for us to watch.

Santiago unbuttoned his Gucci button down shirt and neatly placed it on my night stand, he then stood up and unfastened his Gucci jeans and did the same. I glanced over at him standing on the side of my bed wearing nothing but a wife beater and navy blue Ralph Lauren boxer briefs that looked as though they were made especially for him.

"Damn." I let slip out in a hushed tone.

Santiago looked at me and smiled, "Oh You like what you see?" he asked with a slurred voice.

I don't know if it was the Hennessey or the fact that I had this tall dark piece of chocolate standing in my room half naked, but my pussy instantly began to throb.

Santiago walked over to my side of the bed and grabbed my hand motioning for me to stand up. I stood up in front of him breathing heavily. He reached up and gently let loose the messy bun I had at the top of my head letting my hair fall. He grabbed my face and looked my deep in my eyes before kissing me. I hadn't been touched by a man in so long that I felt as if I was gonna melt in his hands. With the Hennessey suppressing my shyness I ripped his wife beater off him, threw it to the floor and kissed his chest. He pulled the tank top I was wearing over my head as I stepped out of sweat pants. Santiago stopped for a second and looked me up and down standing there in my pink La Perla bra and panty set. He licked his lips and firmly grabbed my ass, lifting me up in to the air. I wrapped my legs around his waist and we fell into a kiss so deep that I don't how I ended up with my back against the wall. He kissed and licked from my neck making a trail with his tongue. My back arched when his tongue found his way to my breast and he gently nibbled my nipples through the lace of my bra. He reached behind me and unclipped my bra and tossed it to the floor and then with one hand slid my panties to the side. He treated my nipples as if they were chocolate Hersey kisses and he devoured them while playing with my clit causing me to moan in extreme pleasure.

"Damn girl!" he whispered "Your pussy wet as hell." My juices had soaked his fingers and was dripping on to the carpet. He licked his fingers and then kissed my lips allowing me to taste my own sweetness. Santiago wrapped his arms around my and carried me over to the bed playfully tossing me on it. He slid my panties off, stepped out of his briefs then climbed on top of me. I glanced down at his dick and my heart skipped a beat. It was so big I got nervous.

"Hold on." I said touching his chest.

"What's wrong baby?" he asked looking me in the eyes.

"I have only been with one nigga and that shit was a long time ago, you are gonna have go slow and be gentle." I proclaimed.

"I got you baby, I promise. I would never hurt you." he said sincerely.

He kissed me again while rubbing the tip of his dick on my clit and then down to my opening. He slowly eased his dick into my tight wet pussy and I gasped for air. Short slow strokes as he pushed inch by inch inside of me. I could feel his dick in the pit of my stomach as he strokes got longer and deeper keeping a slow rhythm. That shit felt so good I felt my body tingling.

"Deeper daddy!" I whispered in his ear as he bit me on my shoulder.

He pushed deeper and a little faster as I tried to match his rhythm. Without warning he pulled out grabbed my ankle and flipped me over on my stomach. He kissed me on the back of my neck then traced my spine with his tongue before biting my butt cheek. Santiago wrapped his massive hands around my petite waist and raised my ass in the air. He didn't waste any time diving right back into my wetness, again slow short strokes at first lead up to long deep strokes that had my head spinning. He reached up and grabbed a handful of my hair and pulled it gently forcing my to left my head up making me scream out. His stokes got deeper and faster causing my juices to drip down my thigh onto the duvet.

"This my pussy now." He voiced as he smacked my ass. All I could do was moan as he was so deep in me I couldn't formulate words. He was pounding my ass so hard that my ass cheeks were bouncing with every thrust. I lost all control of my body as it began to tremble, and I felt that rush coming.

"I'm bout to cum baby!" I said as my legs shook without my permission.

Just as I was right at the peak he pulled his dick out and buried his face in my pussy. I couldn't take it no more, my legs were like wet noodles, unable to hold myself up I screamed "OH GOD!" before collapsing on my stomach. Santiago didn't miss a beat wrapping arms around my thighs, his tongue never leaving my pussy as I tried to squirm away.

"Don't run from me." He said pulling me back to him. He laid on my back being careful not to put all his weight on me. He put his dick back in my dripping wet pussy and whispered in my ear "You gonna have to learn to take this dick. It's yours now." He beginning fucking the shit out of me, he was so deep in me I couldn't catch my breath and just when I couldn't take it anymore we both erupted all over each other.

We both laid their breathing heavy waiting on the room to stop spinning. He looked at me and said "You know you mine now right?" he stated.

"Oh really? So, I have no choice in this matter?" I asked laughing.

"Hell No! Aint no way I'm letting that good pussy get away." He responded.

"Well damn!" I said raising up and looking at him "All I am to you is good pussy?" I asked nudging him playfully.

"No baby, Its everything about you. I have never met a chick that was cool as hell, bout her coin and sexy. You just don't find that too often. And now that I have It's a wrap YOU ARE MINE!" he said leaning in to give me a kiss before rolling off the bed to head to the bathroom.

I laid back smiling looking at the ceiling trying to wrap my head around what had just transpired, before I knew it I had dozed off.

I woke up to the trap phone ringing on my night stand. I looked over at Santiago and he was knocked out, didn't even budge. I climbed out the bed, grabbed the phone and headed to the bathroom, trying not to wake him.

"Good Morning," I said answering the phone on the last ring.

"Hola Senorita!" Angelo responded sounding like he had been woke for hour hours. "I would like to invite you to my estate. I have some things I would like to talk to you about."

"Ok, What time?" I asked wiping sleep out of my eyes.

"I will send a car for at 10:00." He said.

I peeped out the bathroom door and looked at the clock on my night stand, it read 7:13AM.

"Ok I will be ready." I stated.

"Very well see you soon." He responded before ending the call.

I walked out of the bathroom and was startled to find Santiago woke sitting on the side of the bed.

"Good morning." I said walking over to him and kissing him on the forehead.

"Good morning gorgeous, everything ok?" he asked.

"I'm not sure, Angelo says he wants to talk to me about something. He is sending a car for me at 10." I answered sitting down beside him on the bed.

"Oh word!" he reached down and grabbed his pants off the floor. He reached in the pocket and pulled out his trap phone to check it.

"That nigga aint hit me." He said looking confused.

"Maybe he already knew we were together. I mean the man knows everything, we know this." I tried to explain.

"Baby girl, I have known this dude a long time. If he wanted me to come, then he would have made sure that I knew he wanted me there. Angelo doesn't leave nothing up for assumptions he is very specific and direct." He said.

"I feel you." I responded.

By this time, Santiago was getting dressed. I sensed he had caught an attitude about something, so I didn't say a word as I watched him scramble around my room to find his clothes.

"What's wrong?" I finally said.

"Nothing." He said pulling his arms through his shirt. "I'm bout to bounce so you can get ready. Hit me later maybe we can go get dinner or something." He said kissing me on my cheek before turning for the door. "I'll lock the door on my way out."

"Aight, I'll call you when I get back." I said getting up to jump in the shower.

I was showered, dressed and by the time the driver rang the doorbell. I was greeted with a bouquet of red and white roses when I opened the door.

"Good Morning Miss. Jazzell." The Hispanic driver said happily as I stepped out the door. "Let me get that for you." he said referring to the briefcase I was carrying.

"Sure" I said handing to over him.

He escorted me to the Lincoln town car that was running in my driveway and opened the back-passenger door for me to get in. When I slid into the soft leather seat and the door was closed behind me I noticed there was an ice bucket with a bottle of champagne and a glass situated on the floor of the car. The driver opened the door on the other side and placed the briefcase beside me in the seat.

"Would you like a glass of champagne Senorita?" he asked in his deep Spanish accent.

"Sure" I replied, since Santiago and I had been hanging out I had become a regular drinker.

He popped the bottle open, poured me a glass and placed the bottle back in its original resting place. After handing me the full glass he quickly jumped in the driver's seat and we were on our way. I sipped and played around on my phone as we took 52 south the 85 south toward Charlotte. By the time, we had reached Charlotte city limits I had drank over half the bottle and was starting to feel the effects of the alcohol. We drover for another 20 minutes taking Highway 485. I looked out the window and the road sign said Welcome to Ballantyne. We exited the highway and pulled into a gated community where a security guard greeted us. He nodded at the driver and proceeded to open the gate for the car to enter. I was in awe as we rode passed billion dollar homes. I had never seen homes this big in my life, each estate occupied its own block. We pulled into the driveway of what seemed to be the biggest home in the neighborhood and parked. The driver exited the car and ran around to myside to open the door. After helping me out of the car he ran around to the other side to retrieve the brief case. I followed as he leads me up some massive stone stairs and through the huge front double doors. When I stepped into the foyer my mouth dropped.

"WOW! This place is beautiful." I exclaimed looking around.

"Senor Angelo is waiting for you on the terrace. Right this way." He said motioning for me to follow him.

We walked through the massive house and he lead me through some tall French style doors that lead to a huge balcony that overlooked a beautiful courtyard and enormous pool. There was Angelo sitting at a table full of food waiting on me.

"Hola Senorita!" he standing to greet me. "Welcome to my home."

"Hola Senor Angelo, thank you for having me, your home is beautiful." I responded hugging him.

We both sat and the driver placed the briefcase on the table in front of Angelo before rushing off. Angelo popped the brief case open and his face lit up as a smile spread across his face.

"Senorita! What is this?" He asked excitedly.

"That's your cut for this week." I explained proudly.

"How much is it?" he asked holding a stack of bills and flipping through them.

"250K." I answered feeling myself.

"Great job Jazzell, you are definitely Big Johns granddaughter!" he said laughing.

"Well I'm only as good as my team. I can't do it without them and Santiago." I responded

"Indeed, spoken like a true leader." He said proudly.

"And therefore, I wanted to speak with you. I would like to reward you for all of your dedication and hard work." He said sipping his champagne.

"Reward? ...Oh, No senor, no need for a reward. The fact that you came through and helped me feed my family is reward enough." I explained gratefully.

"Yes, I understand. But you have been working so hard. It's time for a vacation. I have arranged a small getaway for you. We fly out to Anguilla tomorrow morning. There we will stay in my estate. You would love it, it makes this place look like a shack." he said.

"Tomorrow?" I asked shocked.

"Si Senorita Tomorrow." He confirmed.

"But I need time to pack, make sure my sisters are good, make sure the block is good." I said frantically.

"Don't worry Senorita everything has been taken care of for you." Angelo explained.

"What about Santiago?" I asked.

"What about him?" Angelo asked with a stern look on his face.

"He has been by myside every step of the way. He is a big reason your return is as it is." I explained.

"You two have grown quite close I see." He stated.

"Yes, we have. He is a good guy." I responded trying to contain my smile.

"Oh, I see." Was his response as he shifted in his seat. "Well sometimes people and things are not as they appear to be."

"What you mean?" I asked puzzled.

"Oh, you will see in time. I try not to sway people opinions of other people, I let them form their own opinions." He responded.

I decided it was best not to ask any more questions. So, I just shrugged and continued to nipple on the food on my plate in front of me. We chit chatted for a little longer about business and life while we ate breakfast and sipped mimosas. After the dishes were cleared from the table, I figured it was time to head back to Winston. I had so much to do before dipping out the country.

"Thank you for breakfast Senor it was truly amazing. But need to be headed back so I can prepare to leave." I stated standing up from my seat.

"Oh no, thank you for coming, it is always a pleasure to have such beautiful company." He replied standing as well with a wide smile.

I felt my pussy throb, it's something about that smile that messes my head up.

"Let me see you out." He said placing his hand on my lower back as we turned toward the double doors. I could feel the hairs all over my body stand at attention. He walked me to the car and opened the door for me.

"I will see you in Anguilla Jazzell." He said kissing me on my cheek before I slid into the backseat.

"See you in Anguilla" I replied and he closed the door.

It took everything in me not to look back as we drove down the long drive way. I can't have a thing for Angelo, that's my Papa connect, he is twice my age and I just started this thing up with Santiago.

"I gotta to shake this shit off." I said to myself shaking my head as if that would make the thoughts fall out. I looked down on the floor and there was a fresh bottle of Champagne in the ice bucket. I grabbed the bottle, popped it, and filled the glass all the way to the brim. I sat back and looked out the window getting lost in my thought of Angelo as we drove the hour and a half back to Winston.

CHAPTER 15

My plane arrived at Clayton J Lloyd Airport in Anguilla around noon the next day. Angelo had a town car waiting for me, the driver quickly put my bags in the trunk and we were off. I had always had my passport but this was my first time flying out of the country. I stared out the car window at the beautiful scenery as we drove to Angelo's estate. After riding for about 15 minutes we arrived at the biggest house I had ever seen in my life, it looked like a castle. We parked and I got out the car to take it all in, I couldn't believe that this is where I was gonna be for the next couple of days. The driver brought my bags in the house and handed it to the butler who then showed me to my room. My room was more like and expensive apartment it was huge. It even had its own wet bar fully stocked with any type of liquor you could think of. The bathroom was the size of my entire bedroom at home, equipped with a gigantic walk in closet, full of designer clothes, shoes, and purses. This closet housed any designer you could think of from Gucci to Oscar de la Renta. I ran my hand over the expensive fabrics in awe.

"Hola Senorita." Angelo said behind me startling me.

"Oh god! You scared me." I said holding my chest.

"I'm sorry Jazzell I didn't mean to scare you." Angelo stated almost laughing.

"This place is beautiful, thank you for having me." I said.

"Thank you for coming, do you like the clothes?" he asked.

"Yes, they are beautiful. Whomever she is definitely has great taste." I said admiring the luxurious threads.

Angelo laughed, "No Senorita, these are for you. Anything you could ever want is already provided for you." he said through chuckles.

"I'm only gonna be here for a few days, this is way too much." I said shocked.

"Well hopefully we can change your mind about that." Angelo said with a winked.

ACE

It had been months since I talked to Jazzy. I know she is hurt that I just got missing on her, but I had no choice, I was backed into a corner, my only options were either go to prison, get killed or leave the country.

I remember that shit like it was yesterday.......

I was on the block on the phone with Jazzy when Juice punk ass pulled up.

Jazzy hung up in my ear just as Juice stepped out the car and walked over to me grinning. Just as I parted my lips to curse him out I notice that Ray was climbing out of the passenger seat of Juice's car. I stood from the stoop I was sitting on and cocked my head to the side.

"What's going on Ray?" asked as he dapped me up.

"I need to talk to you bout some shit fam. Let's take a ride real quick." He said.

I looked at him then at Juice and back at Ray. "Naw fam I aint riding nowhere wit him." I said nodding towards Juice.

Lil Ray looked at Juice, "Yo give us a minute my dude." He said. Juice didn't say anything he just nodded and got in his car. Lil Ray threw his arm around my shoulder and we walked down the block a little.

"Come on brah. You know u good.... I got you. Let's just hear what the nigga has to say." He said.

"Yo! I don't trust that nigga. I don't care what you say. That nigga either working for the police or he working for Towns ,2 motha fukas I don't fuck with. And last I checked you don't either." I stated.

"This nigga been blowing me up for weeks talking bout he got a way for us to make some real bread. Now I already told his ass I don't fuck wit Towns and he claims this has nothing to do with dat nigga." Lil Ray responded.

I thought for a second. "Look the only reason I'm gonna go is to make sure you straight. I aint interested in shit dat nigga got to say." I stated.

"Bet!" Lil Ray replied looking relieved.

"If this nigga even move wrong I'm going to kill his ass" I thought to myself as we walked back to Juice's car. Ray slid in the front as I climbed in the back seat and Juice pulled from the curb and out of the hood. We rode in silence for a little while before I felt like I was about to explode.

"So, what's up?" I asked with venom seeping through my voice.

Juice glared at me in the rearview mirror

"Look brah, you wanted us to hear you out, I'm here, been in the car with you for over 5 minutes and you aint said shit. I aint got all day, there's money to be made." I demanded.

"Yo you aint got to be doing all that yelling in my car dude." He said through clinched teeth.

Lil Ray looked at Juice "Look you said you wanted to holler at me and my nigga, well we here, what's good?" he probed.

Juice took a deep breath and said, "Check it, I got a way for us to make some real dough, straight profit no split. What you make is all yours."

I looked at that nigga like he was crazy, "How?" I asked.

"I got my hands on a few bricks I need help getting off." Juice said.

"So, what in da hell does that have to do with us?" I asked.

"I need help getting this shit off quick. I don't have the clientele yall do." He responded

"So, you just happened to stumble across some free bricks?" I asked skeptically.

"I was in Atlanta a few weeks ago, and ran across this little nigga slipping. I hit him over the head for some dough and a few bricks." Juice replied

I smacked my teeth and said "So that means this nigga comin back looking for his shit and who ever took it!"

"Naw from what I heard the nigga done got locked up and is looking at a 10-year bid." Juice explained.

Lil Ray had been sitting in silence the entire conversation, he finally spoke "Look I don't give a damn where he got the shit from. That's free bricks, free money! If the nigga come back looking for his shit that's on this nigga." he stated pointing at Juice.

There was silence for a minute then I asked "So you just gonna give us the shit? No strings attached. It's just our lucky fuckin day? What's in it for you?" I had a million questions this shit wasn't feeling nor sounding right to me.

"Nigga I said I need help moving it! I aint trying to be sitting on that shit. I need it GONE!" Juice said raising his voice starting to get annoyed.

Lil Ray and I looked at each other. We were always close enough that we know what the other is thinking, and 9 times out of 10 we are usually are on the same page. Up until that point.

"I'm wit it, let's get this dough!" he said dapping Juice up.

My mouth dropped "What?" I yelled looking at him like he had gone bat shit crazy. They both turned and looked at me like I was the one that had lost my mind.

"Yo pull over!" I yelled. "Let me out this mutha fuker, I'll catch an Uber." I said pulling out my cell phone. Juice pulled the car into a Burger King parking lot on Martin Luther King Blvd. I hopped out the car and started walking back towards the hood.

"Yo let me holla at my dude I will hit you later." Lil Ray said before he jumped out the car.

"Yo Ace wait up!" he yelled jogging to catch up with me as Juice pulled out the parking lot and sped off.

I didn't pay him any mind as I set up my Uber to come get me. That nigga had lost his fuckin mind.

"Yo my nigga what's up?" he asked finally stepping beside me.

I stopped in my tracks and turned to him. "Nigga have you lost yo damn mind?"

"Hell NO! but obviously, you have, you know how much of a come up this is?" he asked.

"Only thing you gonna come up with fuckin wit Juice is a toe tag or a case wit da FEDS! Either the nigga who he robbed gonna come lurking or the police cause Juice working for them! Come on man think about it… what nigga you know gonna just hand a nigga some free bands? Especially some nigga that he was once "beefing" wit?" I asked looking Ray dead in the eye.

"I feel you." Ray said looking down at the ground sounded defeated.

"Look I just don't think it's a good move." I stated just as my Uber was pulled into the parking lot of the Chicken & Honey restaurant we were standing in front of.

"Yo you headed back to the hood?" I asked before climbing in the backseat.

"Naw I got to go handle some business I'll hit you later." he responded thumbing through his phone.

"You good? You need me to roll wit you?" I asked.

"Naw I'm good." He replied.

"Cool. I'm bout to go meet Jazzy hopefully her ass aint still mad at me." I said shaking my head.

"Yeah good luck wit dat." He responded laughing. We dapped each other up and went our separate ways.

I had the Uber driver take me to my car that was parked in the hood. As we rode past Jazzys house I couldn't help but smile when I noticed her car wasn't parked in the driveway.

"Good she on her way to meet me!" I thought "I got to make this shit right, I can't lose my girl over dat Tonya bullshit."

I hopped in my car and speed toward the house that the two of us shared. She was already there waiting on me when I pulled into the driveway. I stepped out of the car and walked over to hers to open the door but she had the door locked. The look she gave me through the window was on of hurt and disappointment.

"You aint gonna get out?" I asked through the window. She turned her car off and unlocked the door so I could open it for her to get out. I reached out for a hug and kiss and she turned her head.

"You think you gonna kiss me after you been kissing on that dirty bitch?" she snapped.

I smacked my teeth "Come on baby, you trippin. Let's just go in the house and talk." I pleaded grabbing her hand leading her to the front door. I unlocked the door and we walked in. As soon as I closed the door behind us I grabbed her from behind and pulled her close to me.

"I'm so sorry baby, I swear didn't nothing happened between me and that girl." I stated pleading my case.

She pushed away from me. "How come you didn't tell me then?" She asked looking me square in the eyes.

"I didn't want you to be mad at me." I responded "I was scared you was gonna leave me. Baby she is nothing, she came on to me I was on that liquor I lost my head for a minute" I said still pleading.

"But you had every chance to tell me. You brought me to this house and fucked me while lying to me in the process." She screamed starting to get emotional I could see the tears forming in her eyes.

"Fucked you? I didn't fuck you, you are my girl, I made love to my woman." I yelled back, I could feel myself getting emotional too. I needed to calm down.

"Look" I continued lowering my tone. *"I don't want that bitch I am with who I want. I apologize for not keeping it a hunnid wit you. Damn can we get pass this shit and move on?"* by this point I felt like I was begging.

She stared at me for a few minutes then said *"I don't want you speaking to that bitch ever again. If I see you looking at that hoe I will smack fire out yo ass!"* She exclaimed.

I busted out laughing, *"You know I love it when you talk to me like that."* I said grinning as she tried to keep a straight face.

"I'm serious nigga! And the next time you give a bitch some money she better be a damn jeweler handing you a big ass ring!" she declared, she tried to remain serious but she couldn't help but laugh.

I grabbed her around her waist and pulled her into a deep kiss.

We spent the rest of the weekend in OUR house together, we turned our phones off and secluded ourselves from the rest of the world, I felt like shit was all good again.

Monday morning I woke up before my alarm went off for us to go to school. I looked over at Jazzy sleeping before grabbing my phone and heading downstairs not to wake her. I powered my phone up to check my messages, my phone had been off all weekend so I knew my shit was full. There were a couple of messages from a few of my soldiers, but nothing of importance.

"Damn Ray aint hit me all weekend." I said to myself, *"I will see him in school in a few."* I shrugged and went back upstairs to wake Jazzy.

When we arrived to school I walked Jazzy to her locker.

"Yo have you seen Lil Ray? I hadn't talked to him since my birthday." She asked gathering her stuff for class.

"Last I seen him was Friday before I came to meet you, but only for a second. He claimed he had some business to handle." I replied. pulling my cell phone from my pocket.

"What kind of business? And why didn't you go with him?" She asked.

"He wouldn't tell me Jazzy. I offered to roll wit him but he said he wanted to go solo. Plus, I was coming to meet you." I responded getting a little offended, she acts like I wasn't wit her ass the whole time.

She sucked my teeth, "And you haven't heard from him since?" she reiterated.

"Naw, my phone been off just like yours remember." I stated.

She rolled her eyes.

"I'm gonna text him now and make sure he straight." I said pulling my cell phone from my pocket as the bell rang for 1st period.

"You should've did that last night." she said her voice dripping with attitude.

I looked at her like she was crazy, she was tripping for real.

"Just let me know if you hear from him." she said before kissing me on the cheek slamming her locker door and walking off to class.

I texted Lil Ray and shoved my phone in my pocket before heading to class to start my day. We were in class for about 30 min when there was a knock on the door. I looked up and saw one of the school administrators standing in the hall with a Police Officer. My teacher stepped out of the class for a second and everyone started whispering and speculating on what's was going on.

She came back in and looked dead at me.

"Antoine, would you gather your things and step into the hallway please?" she said.

I felt like the whole class was staring as I gathered my stuff and exited the class.

As soon as I stepped out the door the officer asked "Are you Antoine Knight?"

"Yes" I responded.

"Place the books and bag on the floor, place your hands on your head and turn around." The officer ordered.

"For what?" I asked.

"You have a warrant for your arrest. Now please do as I ask and do not make a scene." The officer demanded.

I did as I was told because for one I was in the middle of the school hallway, and secondly because the way police officers been "accidentally" killing black men, I didn't want to become the next face on the news. The officer searched me and read me my rights as he placed my hands behind my back and handcuffed them. As we were walking up the hall to exit the school, Jazzy came running toward me.

"Baby what's going on?" She asked frantically.

"I don't know. Call my lawyer." I responded looking straight ahead.

"Officer what is he being charged with?" She asked the young black officer that was holding on to my arm.

"Ma'am I need you to back up." Was his response as we pushed past her taking me through the front door of the school and placing me in the back of a police car. I looked back at the school and seen Jazzy staring through the glass at me. I just put my head down as the officer pulled away from the curb and out of the school parking lot. I didn't know if I would see her again I didn't want the expression that was plastered on her face to be the last one I remembered.

We arrived at the police station in no time, it felt like the shortest ride of my life. I was led to a small interrogating room and instructed to sit down after they removed my handcuffs. I sat there for what seemed like an eternity before two detectives entered the room.

"Good morning Mr. Knight, I'm Detective Denosia and this is Detective Bennett" the Hispanic man said as both men sat in the chairs across from me, I looked at both and said nothing.

"Can I call you Ace?" Detective Denosia asked with a crooked smile "Do you know why you are here?"

I shook my head keeping my mouth closed.

Bennett flipped open the folder that was on the desk in front of him, "Do you know this man?" he asked.

I looked at the picture of Big John that was sitting in front of me and looked back at Bennet still saying nothing.

Bennett looked at Denosia and shook his head, "How about this guy?......or him? …. or her?" he asked slamming ore pictures on the table. I looked at the faces of Lil Ray and a few of our soldiers sitting on the table starting back at me, still I said nothing.

"Oh, we gonna play the silent game." Denosia said chuckling. "How about her?" he smirked as he threw one last picture on the table. There was a picture of Jazzy staring at me, in the picture Big John was walking into her house with 2 duffle bags as she held the door open. I stared at the picture for a minute then asked "What do any of them have to do with me?"

"We have reason to believe that you along with these people are involved in the biggest drug ring in Forsyth County." Denosia said staring at me.

"And what makes you think that?" I asked staring back at him.

"We have had our eye on Big John and his operation for a while now." Bennett stated. "Now you either gonna get in front of this thing and let us help you or you going to prison for a long time."

"On what charges?" I laughed.

"What charges? How about drug trafficking and distributing!" Bennett yelled back.

I sneered at him.

"How about murder!" Bennett yelled tossing yet another picture on the table. Staring back at my deep into my soul was the man I shot years ago, for stealing from Big John. I couldn't take looking at him, I had to look away.

"Do you remember him?" Bennett asked sliding the picture closer to me.

"Naw I don't know that nigga." I said shaking my head.

"That's funny cause your homeboy told us something different." Denosia claimed.

"What fuckin homeboy?" I asked.

"Rayshawn Harris or Lil Ray so yall call him." Denosia stated.

I wanted to spit in his face but instead I looked at him and said calmly, "I really don't want to hear nothing else, you can tell all this bullshit to my lawyer once he gets here."

Denosia pulled out a small stack of papers and slid them over to me. "We'll give you a minute to read over these statements… while we wait on your lawyer". He sneakered as him and Detective Bennet stood and exited the room.

I thumbed through the papers in front of me. As I read the words on the paper I felt sick to my stomach. Apparently, Lil Ray had gotten caught up with a confidential informant and had made a deal with the feds to bring the whole organization down to save his own ass. The statement that he signed named everyone from Big John, to the foot soldiers, to the corner boys. He even had his aunts and uncles named in the paperwork. There was a complete breakdown about how the organization was ran including drop off and pick up times and locations. I couldn't believe what I was *reading. At the end of the document there was his signature as well as the name of the confidential informant, Duwan Burton.*

"I KNEW IT!!" I screamed clearing all the papers from the table in one sweep. I knew that nigga Juice was on some bullshit. But I couldn't believe Lil Ray though, that was my brother, my partner, seeing his name on those statements broke my heart. I took a deep breath and sat down putting my head on my hands trying to think of my next move.

My lawyer arrived just as I was about to go crazy in that little room.

"How are you doing Mr. knight?" he asked as he sat down.

"To be honest not so good. What can we do to get me outta this?" I asked shaking my head.

"From the looks of things, it seems as though they have enough evidence for a strong case against you." he said.

"Look get Judge Toleman on the phone. He can get me outta this." I demanded.

"Already done, he is working on it now." My lawyer confirmed.

I had a few politicians and members of the courts in my pockets. They are loyal clients that spent good money with me, and in exchange for my discreetness something as simple as a traffic ticket wont even make it past the filing clerks desk.

"What about Miss. Harris and her cousin?" He asked.

"What you mean?" I asked looking at him like he was crazy.

"They were brought in for questioning as well. They are in interrogation as we speak.

"Can you take care of them for me. I can handle these assholes. Are you sure Judge Toleman is working on it?" I asked.

"Yes, he is. We should be hearing back from him any minute." He responded.

"Ok well get my girl and her cousin up outta here now." I demanded.

"I gotcha." He responded getting up from his seat and exiting the room.

It seemed like an eternity before the 2 detectives returned to the room and sat down, the room was silent for a few moments.

"Look we can work it so that these charges on you can disappear," Bennet said looking at me. "But contingent on the information you give us and your cooperation to help us."

"My cooperation?" I asked bewildered.

"Yes, if you can give us more information on Big Johns organization so that we can build a strong case against him." Denosia said. "With that we can grant you complete immunity."

I couldn't help but laugh. "Yall done lost yall mind? That's not how I get down dog." I said still laughing.

"So, I guess you going to prison." Denosia exclaimed.

"Naw that's not gonna happen either." I responded.

"How can you be so sure?" Bennet asked.

Just as I was about to answer there was a knock on the door. A black officer poked his head and summoned the 2 officers to the hallway. When they returned, they looked as if they were gonna cry.

"I guess you have some friends in some very high places." Denosia stated. "Mr. Knight, you are free to go."

I jumped up out of my chair and my lawyer and I was outta that building in the blink of an eye.

"Come on Ace I will give you a ride to car." My lawyer said.

A soon as we got in the car he said "Miss. Harris and her cousin have been released and are home."

"Good" I responded.

"Judge Toleman would like to see you." he continued.

"Cool I will go see him tomorrow." I responded.

"No, he wants to see you tonight." He explained.

"I guess I aint got no choice." I said shrugging.

When we got to the Judge's home he was sitting in his office.

"Good evening Mr. Knight." He said as we entered the room and closed the door behind us.

"Good evening, what's going on?" I asked.

"Have a seat." He responded pointing to the empty chair in front of his desk.

"So, what was so important that couldn't wait till tomorrow?" I asked sitting down.

"Well as we both know Big Johns organization has been shut down." He started.

"Yes ok, so is there anything you can do to get him out?" I asked.

"I'm not interested in getting Big John out. I'm already in debt for getting you cleared." Judge Toleman stated.

"What you mean?" I asked.

"Well you have some serious charges facing you, including murder. I had to call in some major people to make those charges go away." He said.

"Ok and?" I said.

"Well one of those major people was Mayor Taylor, and in return for getting you off you have to agree to a few terms." He responded.

"What terms? Did he forget that half his salary goes up his noise? Shouldn't me keeping my mouth closed about that be good enough?" I said.

Judge Toleman shifted in his seat and cleared his throat. "Apparently, it's not." he said.

"Well what else do he want?" I questioned getting aggravated.

"He wants you to leave Winston Salem." He finally said.

"WHAT?" I yelled.

"With one of the of the biggest drug organization being shut down during his time in office and this being election year, he doesn't want to take any chances, he wants you out of the city." Toleman said straight forwardly.

"What in the hell I have to do with the fucking election?" I asked confused.

"Well who's to say you are not getting ready to take over Big Johns organization? The mayor just doesn't want that in his city especially during election time." He answered. "If you stay you go back to jail and face the same fate as Big John."

I thought for a second and the room was silent.

"I have to leave for good" I asked bewildered.

"No, just until after the trial and election are over." he answered. "But when you come back, you have to make sure you remain below he radar."

"Ok I will get my things in order and be gone by the weekend." I said.

"No, he wants you gone by sunrise." Toleman corrected.

"By sunrise?" I yelled "That's impossible!"

"Well make it possible, if not there will be a warrant issued for your arrest. We already have your plane ticket and housing set up for you. The mayor has made sure that your accommodations are to your standards in exchange for you to keep his little secret." He explained.

"I guess I have no choice, I just have to get my girl and we will be gone by morning." I responded defeated.

"Unfortunately, you can't take your girlfriend. No one can know about this deal or that you are gone. That voids the agreement and again you will go to jail." Toleman retorted.

I felt like my head was spinning, I can't even say goodbye to Jazzy. What will she think?

"Hold up, when Big John sees that I am not locked up, he is gonna think I snitched on him, then I will be a dead man. No matter where I go in this country, he will find me, his reach is long" I exclaimed.

"Well that brings me to my next thing." Toleman said.

"What now? What else could it be damn?" I yelled.

"Not only do you need to Leave Winston Salem we need you to leave the country." He responded.

"Leave the country?... and go where?" I asked.

"Anguilla." He answered.

"Anguilla?" I shouted. "what the fuck am I supposed to do in Anguilla?"

"That's none of my business. Do what you been doing here." Toleman answered smugly.

Chapter 16

Now here I am in Anguilla and have been for the past 4 months. Alone.... I couldn't even log into my social media accounts, no Facebook, no Instagram, nothing. It's like I disappeared. It took everything in me not to call Jazzy. But once all this is over I'm sure that we can pick back up like we were never apart. At first I stayed to myself, I only left the house when I had to. I didn't try to meet or get to know anybody. But after about 2 weeks I started feeling restless I decided to get out and venture the city on night. I stumbled across a bar and I went in to have me a drink. It was small and raggedy but I liked it. So, it quickly became my new hang out spot. I got cool with the bartenders as well as the owner.

On night I was sitting at the bar per usual when a Hispanic man walked in. I could tell this man was someone of importance because the entire mood in the room changed. Everyone seemed to admire and fear him at the same time. He walked in and took the seat directly beside me and the bartender quickly pour him a drink without being asked.

"How are you?" he looked at me and asked with a deep Spanish accent.

"I'm cool." I responded and turned my attention back to my drink.

"Welcome to Anguilla Ace." He said staring at me with a straight face.

The sound of my name made me spin in my seat toward him.

"Do I know you?" I asked searching his face for some sort of recognition.

"Sort of" he responded.

He extended his hand for me to shake it "My name is Angelo. I'm a friend of Big Johns." He stated.

My mouth hit the floor. I had heard Big John speak his name but I had never met him. At one point

Ray and I used to call him *The Ghost* because it's like he was always there but was never seen. A million thoughts were going through my mind, *"Does Big John think I snitched? Was he here to kill me? How did he find me here?"*

I just sat there bewildered not knowing what to say.

"Can we speak in the back office please?" Angelo asked standing up from his seat and straighten his jacket.

"Cool" was all I could muster as I stood as well and followed him to a small office in the back of the bar.

"Have a seat." He said as he propped his self against the edge of a small wooden desk.

I sat as I was instructed and remained silent.

"So, what brings you to my country my friend?" Angelo asked,

"I'm on vacation." I responded.

"On vacation? A vacation sponsored by Mayor Coles?" he probed raising his eyebrow.

I remained silent.

"Look before you even insult me with a lie I'm going to answer for you." Angelo stated. "You got arrested when Big John got knocked but instead of going to jail you worked out a deal with the Mayor where if he gets you off you will leave the country. Am I correct?" he asked.

"Yeah that's right." I answered.

"You are a very smart and savvy young man. It is always in your best interest to have a few politicians in your pocket, especially in our line of work. I used to tell Big John that all the time, but he didn't think it was necessary" He explained.

"Thank you. I agree." I responded.

"So, my next question is how long?" he quizzed.

"Until the trial is over and the Mayor gets re-elected." I returned.

"Well I have a proposal for you." Angelo baited.

"Yeah what's that?" I threw back.

"I want you to work for me." He stated. "You can handle shit here for me in Anguilla and when you are able to return to the states you can run your own organization. I'm looking to expand, I want to take over the entire city of Winston Salem and the surrounding areas."

I couldn't help but smile. Secretly this was a dream come true, I would have the best connect and the best product in the city. I thought for a minute then said., "We both know that Big John is not gonna just lay down and let me take over his territory." I explained.

"Don't nothing move in that city without me. I have a great respect for Big John but at the end of the day I am still his boss. Besides you wouldn't be taking over Big John's territory. I have someone in place for that. I plan to shut Towns down." Angelo revealed.

"I'm wit it." I responded. I know that even though I had been gone for months I could always jump back in and do my thing, this hustling shit is all I know, it's in my blood.

He looked down at the floor "It's going be heart breaking when Big John finds out his own grandson is the one that put the final nail in his coffin." He said solemnly, shaking his head.

I looked at him astonished, "How do you know that?" I asked.

Angelo laughed as he raised from the corner of the desk and walked over to the other side and sat in the leather chair behind the desk.

"I know everything, I knew you were coming before you knew." He stated. "Not only did he turn his family in he also stole all of my product out of Big Johns house before the Feds raided it. That's why there were no drugs found in the house." He added.

"Damn!" I was shocked. "I can't believe he stooped that damn low."

"I am not surprised, truthfully you shouldn't be either. You have known him for years, you know he is flashy and greedy, a dangerous combination."

"Yeah you right about that." I agreed.

"We both know that because of his unloyalty he has to be taken care of." He stated.

"I understand." I replied. I could feel a lump forming in my throat, I was still fucked up behind the betrayal, but I didn't want Ray to die.

"That needs to be taken care of right away, he is lucky I let him live this long." He said staring me in my eyes. "And you need to do it."

"What?" I yelled, I must have heard wrong.

"Ace, you will quickly learn that I do not repeat myself." He said sternly.

I stood up and walked over to his desk "How am I supposed to do that when I'm stuck here?" I asked. "I don't even know where he is."

"My sources tell me that he is living in Atlanta, and have made quite a name for himself, off my product that he stole of course." He said.

"Ok ...and? ..... again, how am I supposed to do that when I can't go to the states?" I asked.

"I have gotten word from my source that he will be arriving in the Dominican Republic Friday. I would love for him not to make it back." Angelo expressed.

I am hardly ever speechless, but it seems lately that a lot of shit have been taking me by surprise lately.

"Look I grew up with that man, if it wasn't for him and his family I don't know where I would be. It's not easy for me to agree to just end his life." I explained.

"If it wasn't for him you would be still in your city, making money, building a life with that beautiful girlfriend of yours." Angelo responded.

"You're right." Was all I could say.

"Look I like you a lot Ace, and I understand Ray is like a brother to you. But you got to understand that's part of the game. Any unloyalty must be handled. You live be the sword you die by the sword, that's just the way it goes."

I shook my head and remained silent because I knew he was right.

I awoke to my doorbell ringing. I looked over at the clock on the night stand, it read 8:13 AM.

"Who the hell is this?" I asked myself as I grabbed my gun from under my pillows and headed to the door. I looked through the peephole and noticed it was Angelo, I immediately unlocked and opened the door.

"Good morning my friend." Angelo said as he walked through the door.

"Yeah, what up." I replied closing and locking the door behind him.

He walked through the house, straight to the kitchen, grabbed the bottle of Tequila that was on the counter and sat at the island. I followed behind, grabbed two glasses out of the cabinet and sat beside him. Angelo poured us both a shot and without speaking a word we touched our glasses together before throwing back the shots.

"You ready?" he asked breaking the silence.

"Nope." I replied pouring another shot.

"Plane leaves tonight, you will be taking my private jet." He stated.

"I'll be there." I responded throwing the liquor down my throat.

"I've made a reservation at the hotel that he is staying at, just give them my name and they will give you a key." He informed.

"Ok cool. So how am I supposed to do this?" I asked

"There is a girl with him, she will text your phone when he has fallen asleep. She will let you in his room and you take care of the rest." He responded. "You must come back tonight and bring the girl back with you." Angelo instructed.

"Ok". Was my only reply as I poured yet another drink. I needed this liquor to numb my body and my mind to get through this.

We sat and drank for a few more minutes before Angelo left. The rest of the day I seemed to be moving in slow motion. I finished the entire bottle before I realized that no amount of liquor could prepare me for what I was about to do.

At 7 o'clock on the dot Angelo's driver picked me up and drove me to a jet that was waiting my arrival. I continued to throw back shots of Tequila throughout the entire flight. Once we landed I checked into the hotel and awaited the text as instructed. It wasn't until 2:15 AM my phone dinged alerting me that it was time. When I arrived at the room door it was slightly open as Angelo said it would be. I peeked in and seen Ray was passed out on the bed naked. I kept my gun by myside as I made my way further into the room. The girl never made eye contact with me as she hurriedly got dressed. The small room smelled of pussy and sex and there was cocaine and liquor bottles everywhere. I walked over to the bed and stood there for a second to build my courage. I grabbed a pillow off the bed, put it over Ray's face, and pointed the ended of my silencer at its intended target. I closed my eyes and pulled the trigger and just like that.... Lil Ray was gone. I could feel a single tear sneak down my face and I didn't even bother to wipe it.

When I opened my eyes the girl was standing by the door staring at me.

"You ok?" she asked.

"Yeah I'm cool." I lied.

"Let's get outta here" was her response as she opened the door, peaked her head out and looked up and down the hallway before stepping out.

I tucked my gun in my pants and was out the door right behind her.

We used a side door to exit the hotel where there was a car waiting to take us back to Angelo's plane.

"You sure you ok?" she asked once we were seated and prepared to take flight.

"Not really but I will be aight." I replied.

"So, what's your name?" she asked.

The look I gave her should've told her that I wasn't in the mood for small talk.

"My name is Tiffany, but everyone calls me Tip." She continued.

"Ace" I said resting my head back on the head rest and closing my eyes.

She must have gotten the hint because she turned in her seat and remained quiet for the rest of flight.

In no time, we were landing in Anguilla where there were 2 cars waiting on for us. I helped her with her bag and we went our separate ways.

Once I got home I took a long hot shower hoping that the image of my best friends' brains blown out would wash down the drain along with this sadness and guilty feeling. I have never felt like this before and I have no one here with me.

CHAPTER 17

JAZZELL

After I got settled in I slipped on a sexy bathing suit and went to soak in some sun by the pool. It was the first time in a long time I could take a step back from life and think.

I had been so wrapped up in Santiago and getting money, I forgot about my reason for all this. I still hadn't talked to my cousin Lil' Ray, it's like he just vanished in thin air. I hadn't been to see my family in weeks, I just sent money and paid the lawyers. I had no idea what was going with their case. I barely see my sisters and cousin because I'm always ripping and running. They have everything they could want or need but my time. I keep forgetting the fact that they lost their family too. It was time to get back on my shit.

I stayed in Anguilla for a week and it was the best time of my life. I sat around all day and his staff waited on me hand and foot, anything I wanted I got. Angelo would be gone most of the day but he spared no expense to make sure my stay was amazing. Everyday there was some sort of gift laying around for me, from shoes, to clothes, to jewelry. But it was a bit much for me.

The look of lust in Angelo's eyes when he looks at me makes me uneasy. Yes, he is one of the sexiest men I have seen in my life and he is filthy rich but he is my Papa's connect. I know that's a line I can't cross. Besides, Santiago and I just really made it official, I don't want to mess that up.

The day before I was due to leave Angelo came home and told me to get dressed cause we were going to dinner. On the way to the restaurant, he told me he had someone that he wanted me to meet. We arrived at a beautiful restaurant that was right on the beach and was seated quickly. Not long after we were seated, a young woman was escorted to our table. Angelo stood to hug and kiss her on the cheek before turning to introduce us.

"Jazzell this this is Tiffany. She will be joining us for dinner." He stated.

"Nice to meet you Tiffany," was my response as Angelo pulled her chair out and she slid in the seat beside me.

"Nice to meet you too." She responded smiling.

Looking at her could not tell her Ethnicity. She had the body of a black woman with plump hips, full breast, and a round ass. Her skin look like soft smooth caramel. Her hair though it wasn't as what we consider "good hair", was long and thick and had a shine as if she just walked out the salon. She had almond shaped eyes that complimented her round face and dimples. She was almost breath taking.

I was taken aback when she finally spoke after being seated at the table for a few minutes. She spoke Spanish fluently. She and Angelo had an entire conversation in their native language, I almost felt as though they forgot I was at the table until Angelo looked at me.

"Would you like a glass of champagne?" he asked me.

"Yes please." I responded.

He summoned the waiter over to our table and ordered a bottle of champagne.

"My reason for bringing you two beautiful ladies together is one that I'm sure the both of you would appreciate." He stated as the waiter scurried away.

Tiffany and I both looked at each other then back at him.

"Jazzell I am very proud of you. You have claimed your grandfathers throne as your own and are running a successful organization with class and grace. You have locked down the East and South side and everyone on your team is happy." He said smiling.

"Thank you." I responded smiling as well.

"Tiffany," he said looking at her, "You have been riding with me for many years. You have handled task for me that some may seem impossible. I appreciate all the work you put in for me and I think it's time for a promotion." He stated.

"A promotion?" she reiterated.

"Yes." He continued. "I'm ready to expand. Right now, Towns is running the West and North side and I want it all."

I shifted in my seat at the sound of Towns name.

"How are we going to do that?" I asked. "Towns has a major connect that no one knows. If he got it people are gonna buy it. The only way I see us taking his territory is by force. And that's gonna cause a lot if friction."

Angelo looked at me a smiled "You are absolute right and that's what I plan to do. I will convince most of his workers to work for me and the ones that don't will just have to lay down, including Towns" he explained.

"But what about his connect. I mean, he not just gonna let you stop his money like that." I responded.

Angelo and Tiffany both laughed.

"I see you haven't fully grasped who I am. His connect is the least of my worries." He stated.

"As I was saying." He continued. "I have someone that I am going to put in place to run Towns' territory but I need Tiffany to be the face. Everyone comes through you. No one goes directly to him, but you do not make a decision or a move without him, understood?"

"Yes, I understand." She responded obediently.

"Jazzell I need you and Tiffany to be my Queens in this game. Just like in chess the Queens are the most important and deadliest piece on the board. You have to protect your King and your Kingdom at all cost." Angelo instructed.

The two of us sat there listening intensely like school girls in a classroom being instructed.

"Jazzell you already have a strong team but I need your help putting a team together for Tiffany. The queen is only as strong as the pawns that protect her." Angelo stated.

We both nodded in unison as he continued.

"When you get back to the states tomorrow we will begin to make moves to make this shit happens. I hope you ladies are ready for the takeover." He said laughing.

We enjoyed our dinner and we all three went back to Angelo's estate. I went to my room to shower and change into a swimsuit. I wanted to get one more dip in his luxurious pool before I head back to reality the next day.

As I was walking toward the pool I walked past Angelo's office. The door was cracked open and I could over hear he and Tiffany talking. I moved closer to the door the get a better listen.

"How are you coming with that mark?" he asked.

"It's coming along smoothly. He is falling for me like we knew he would." She said laughing.

"Good. Just keep him entertained a little longer I want him to really trust you." Angelo said.

"Ok no problem." she responded.

"In a few weeks suggest that you go on a trip together. Let him pick the place. Once we get him out of the country then we will make our move." Angelo instructed.

"Cool. I could use another getaway." Tiffany responded and they both laughed.

I hurried up and got away from the door before I was caught ear hustling. After taking a dip in the pool I took a shower, packed my things, and went to bed to get some rest for my early flight home. I couldn't wait to see Santiago and I truly missed my sisters and cousin.

I arrived home around 10AM and was blown away when I walked through the door. There were roses and rose petals everywhere. I followed the trail from the living room upstairs to my bedroom. When I open the double doors, I thought I would see Santiago waiting for me. But instead I found my bed filled to the brim with shopping bags. From Farragamo, La Perla, Victoria Secret you name to it was there. I pulled out my phone and called him grinning the entire time.

"What's up?" he answered on the second ring.

"Hey you. what you doing?" I asked.

"You already know…. Handle business." He stated dryly.

"Oh ok. I just touched down. I figured you would be here." I said confused. He seemed to have an attitude.

"Well somebody had to run shit while you were on vacation. The grind don't stop." He barked.

"Yo what's wrong with you?" I asked, my attitude was started to stir up.

"Nothing I'm good." He threw back at me.

"Well anyway. I called to let you know I am home and to thank you for all the gifts." I wasn't getting ready to pacify him cause he in a mood.

"What gifts?" he probed.

"What do mean what gifts? …. The roses and rose petal, the bed full of shopping bags." I responded puzzled.

"Yo I wish I could take the credit for that. But that wasn't me shorty." He replied.

"What you mean?" I asked walking over to bed and rummaging through the bags.

"It wasn't me! I hadn't been to your house since you left and I damn sure ain't bought nothing! That's that other nigga you fucking with!" He sneakered.

I noticed a note laying on my pillow:

Jazzell,

Thank you for a wonderful week. It was amazing having you here. You enjoyed your wardrobe here so much that I felt you should have the same at home.
Sincerely,

Angelo

I stood there with the phone to my ear shocked for a moment.

"You cheating on me already?" Santiago laughed breaking me out of my trance.

"Of course not." I responded.

"Well who are they from?" he probed.

"Angelo." I admitted, regretting telling him as soon as the name left my lips.

"Angelo!" he yelled "Why the fuck is Angelo buying you shit? You must've gave him some pussy!"

"What you just say?" I yelled back.

"You heard me! You must've fucked him. Why in the hell else would he be buying you shit?" he shouted in the phone.

"First, this is not community pussy, I don't just give pussy away. Once I fuck with you there is nobody else!" I shouted back. I was offended.

"Well it's something. A man doesn't just buy a woman shit unless he done hit it and want some more or he is trying to hit it!" he retorted.

"That's my connect. I don't mix business and pleasure." I stated.

"You did with me!" was his response. "Plus, that man is rich. Everybody got a price."

By this point I was pissed. "Let me tell you something Santiago, my pussy nor my soul is for sale. I don't fuck for money I know how to make my own dough. But that's something you know already!" I said.

"What in the hell is that supposed to mean?" he asked.

"Nigga be real. You aint never seen this much money in yo life! You were already on, but I took you to another level!" I boasted.

"Oh, that's how you feel huh?" he asked chuckling.

"Yep!" I threw back at him.

There was a moment of silence.

"Look both of us are getting upset I don't want to argue with you. I will swing by later." He said lowering his voice.

"Yeah whatever!" I said before hanging up the phone.

"He got me fucked up!" I said to myself looking at my watch. It was 10:30, I needed to get a move on if I was gonna make it to the jail by 11. I grabbed my keys and purse and rushed out the door.

CHAPTER 18

I arrived to the jail and was signed in by 11:00. I sat at the table waiting for my Papa to escorted to the visiting room. I know he is going to get in my shit for not coming to see him for weeks.

I heard the door open and he and my uncle Troy walked I, both in handcuffs and shackles. The guard uncuffed them before they sat at the table in front of me.

"Hey baby girl!" my Papa said smiling.

"Hey Papa! Hey Unc! How are you guys doing?" I asked.

"Everything is everything" was my uncles' response.

"I hear you are doing great things." My Papa said smiling.

I couldn't help but smile proudly. "Yeah everything is running smoothly." I said.

"Good, have you heard from your cousin?" Uncle Troy asked looking worried.

"No I haven't it's like he and Ace fell off the face of the earth." I responded.

The men looked at each other and back at me.

"Baby girl I have something to tell you." my Papa said.

"What's going on?" I asked. I could tell by the sound of his voice it was good.

"We received our Discovery Packet from the lawyers last week." Uncle Troy started "And it's not good."

"Ok... so what it say?" I asked frantically.

"Your cousin snitched on us.... The whole family! He wrote statements and everything. He is testifying against us on trial." My Papa said. I could see the tears forming in his eyes.

"WHAT?" I yelled "That's impossible. That can't be right!"

"Its true Jazzy." My uncle said lowering his head in shame.

"Apparently, he got caught up with an informant and gave us up to save his own ass." My Papa informed.

"So, who in the hell is the informant?" I asked.

"Somebody name Dewan Burton." He answered.

"Juice!" I yelled.

"Oh, you know him?" my uncle Troy asked surprisingly.

"Yes, and you do too, that was Tan's boyfriend. That guy she was dating right before all this shit went down." I retorted.

The men gave each other a look of shock then threw it back my way.

"So, what about Ace?" I asked.

"Nothing in our discovery mentions Ace at all. The lawyers said they have a few pictures of him but it's all circumstantial. He wasn't seen doing anything illegal." Big Johns said. "So maybe he just left the city to lay low because shit was hot."

"Naw Papa it's something else. He would've at least told me." I said. "I have been to his apartment, it looks like he hasn't been there in months."

"Well as of now the lawyers are saying that don't have a strong case against us because there were no drugs found at all, just money. The entire case is standing on the testimony of Ray and this Juice character." Uncle Troy explained.

"Have all spoke to Aunt Tissie? I'm sure his Mama can talk him out of this nonsense." I said shaking my head.

"I had your cousin go visit her to see if she had heard or spoke to Ray and she hadn't." Big John said.

"Look you have to find him. He will listen to you. Make sure he don't testify." Uncle Troy demanded.

"Yes sir. I will do everything I can." I responded.

"And get one of your soldiers on that Juice dude. We go to trial in a month, he needs to be taken care of immediately! Big John demanded.

"Yes sir" was all I could say.

"We are proud of you baby girl. You are holding this family down and keeping our name good in the streets. I know it feels like a lot but we need you to be strong. Even though I'm still the head of this family, right now you are the neck. The head can't move without the neck." He explained.

"Yes sir." I said again.

"When you come back next week I need some good news." He said raising up from the table, my uncle following his lead.

"Ok." I said sounding like a defeated child.

Uncle Troy looked at me "Lift your dam head up!" he barked. "Don't you walk outta here with your head down like a wounded puppy. You hold your head high and carry yourself like the Princess we raised you to be."

I took a deep breath and stood up lifting my head high.

"That's better. We love you, see you next week." He said smiling and kissing me on the cheek. I forced a smile as they walked out the room.

When I got home, Tan was sitting at the table eating a sandwich.

"What's up cuz? When you get back?' she asked in between bites.

"This morning. I just left from seeing Papa and your dad." I stated sitting at the table across from her.

"Oh yeah, is that why you look like you just got a spanking?" she said laughing.

"Yeah, I got an ear full today." I responded.

"So, what's going on?" she asked.

"They got their Discovery from the lawyers the other day." I started.

"What the hell is a Discovery?" she asked.

I looked at her like she had two heads, "bitch did you pay attention at all in school?" I teased.

She smacked her teeth and rolled her eyes.

"A Discovery Packet is basically a packet that has all the evidence the Feds have against you and what they are going to use to prosecute you in trial. It has any pictures, recordings or statements signed by witness." I explained.

"Oh, so now they know who snitched on them?" she asked.

"Exactly!" I responded.

"So, who is it?" she probed.

I took a deep breath and said "Lil Ray and Juice."

"Stop fucking play, that's not funny. Who is it for real?" she reiterated.

"I'm not fucking joking! I'm dead as serious!" I shouted.

"What the fuck? Why? How? ... When?" she threw at me dropping her sandwich and leaning back in the chair with her mouth wide open.

"Girl I don't know. Now they want me to find both of them." I said.

"What you mean find? And then what?" she asked almost yelling.

"They want us to talk Ray outta testifying and have Juice killed." I responded.

"Jazzy you know that if Papa don't take care of Lil Ray then Angelo will." She uttered.

"Tan I know, I been thinking about this all the way home. Even if we do get him to not testify, he still went against code. He has to go." I could feel the tears forming in my eyes as I spoke.

Tan got up and walked over to me and wrapped her arms around me, hugging me tight.

"Jazzy that's my cousin too and I love him dearly. But he broke the code, it's part of the game." She said.

She let me go and grabbed some tissues out the kitchen so I could wipe my face. She sat back down and pushed her plate to the middle of the table.

"I done lost my damn appetite." She said. "I need a drink."

"Yeah me too." I agreed as she got up to go to the kitchen.

She returned with a bottle of Jose' Cuevo and 2 shot glasses.

"We got to come up with a plan on how we gonna find Ray before Angelo finds out and how we gonna get Juice. This is personal I want to be there when Juice gets what's coming to him." she declared.

"I feel you." I said pouring me a shot and tossing it down my throat.

Just then it hit me.

"I got it!" I yelled jumping up from my seat to grab my purse.

"What?" Tan asked startled.

I fumbled through my purse until I found my phone.

I didn't respond as I scrolled through my contacts. I found the number I was in search of and placed the call.

She answered on the second ring "Hola Jazzell." She said in her sweet voice.

"Hola Tiffany. I need your help." I exclaimed.

"Sure" she said. "What's up"

"We going to have to meet up, you know I can't do this phone shit." I responded.

"Cool. I can be in the city tomorrow. Text me your address." She responded.

"Ok, I'm sending it right now." I responded.

I hung up the phone and texted her before placing my phone on the table.

"Are you gonna tell me what the hell is going on?" Tan asked looking lost.

"We gonna put Tiffany on Juice. If anybody can find him, it's her." I stated.

"And then what?" she asked.

"You know niggas get stupid when pussy is involved. We will have her take him to a hotel or something. Then we get the goons to run up in there and murk his ass off." I explained.

"What about Ray?" she quizzed.

"That's fam, at the end of the day I'm not sending nobody after my cousin. I must figure out a way to take care of that myself." I answered.

"I just wanna be there when that nigga Juice get his. I got to see the look on his face." She spoke slightly smiling.

"You crazy as hell you know that!" I shouted and we both burst into laughter

It took 2 weeks for Tiffany to find Juice, his stupid ass was "laying low" in a cheap motel in Clemmons, a little town right outside of Winston-Salem. I don't know how she found him but I do know it took her no time to get him to invite her to his hotel room. She texted me the location and I called a couple of my goons to let them know it was time. Later that night Tan and I along with my two henchmen went to pay him a visit. When we got to the hotel we waited until the parking lot was quiet and there was minimal movement. Around 2AM Tiffany texted me our code word letting me know it was time to come up. When we reached the entrance to the room the door was slightly open and we all filed in quietly. He room smelled of stale cigarettes and hot sexy. We could hear the shower run as Juice was washing the sweat from fucking him. I sat on the bed, Tan leaned against the wall and my two soldiers stood by the door. Tiffany got dressed and was out the door by the time Juice turned the water off stepped out of the shower.

"Roll another blunt!" He yelled from behind the closed door of the bathroom. We all remained silent.

"Did you hear ....4" he started to ask as he stepped out the bathroom with a towel around his waist. When he seen us he stopped mid -sentence.

"What's up Juice man?" Tan said smiling.

"You what the hell all doing in my room?" he yelled.

"Stop all that yelling and put some fuckin pants on nigga!" one of my soldiers yelled back, picking up Juices' pants from the floor and tossing them at him.

Juice turned around to slide his pants on.

"Aww nigga don't act like I aint ever seen it before!" Tan said laughing.

"Whatever" he threw over his shoulder, "What yall want?" he asked.

"Don't play stupid, you know why we are here." I said calmly.

"Look, I don't get shit to do with yo Papa getting knocked. That was all your cousin." He started explaining.

"Don't be trying to plea now." Tan spit at him

"It was his idea. He wanted to steal Big Johns dope then get him knocked off and take over." Juice broke down.

"Shut the fuck up!" I yelled getting angry. "You a fuckin rat ass bitch. Keep my cousin name out yo mouth!"

Juice looked at me then at Tan, "I'm the rat but you gave me all the information I needed to take your family down!" he shouted at her.

We all turned and looked at Tan.

"You're a fuckin lair!" she shouted.

"Yo Jazzy, I don't mean no harm, but we in a cheap as motel with paper thin walls. Yall doing too much talking. Let's do what we came to do and bounce." Tank, one of my soldiers stated.

"You are absolutely right." I said standing up and walking to the door. "Do him in" I commanded and made my exit.

By the time, I made it downstairs and was unlocking the car, Tan and the two goons were speed walking behind me.

"Hurry up let's get the hell outta here!" Chuck, the other soldiers said as we piled in to the car.

"Dam that was quick!" I exclaimed after we sped out of the parking lot and was taking the ramp to get on to I-40 east.

"We don't waste no time. The longer you take the more chances of some bullshit happening.... get in, get it done and get out." Chuck explained.

"Yo cuz! I never seen anybody get shot like that. Not up close and person. It gave me a rush!" Tan exclaimed grinning from ear to ear.

"Yo I think we have created a monster!" Tank laughed.

"Hell yeah!" I exclaimed "Now let's go eat, I'm starving."

The shit Juice said kept playing in my head, what the fuck did he mean? What information had Tan given him? I looked over at her and she was zoned outlooking out the window daydreaming. I would have to address it later when we are alone.

CHAPTER 19

With all the commotion, I hadn't really spent any time with Santiago. He has been acting shady since I got back from Anguilla. We spoke everyday but it was just about business. When it was time for us to count the money, and deliver Angelo his cut, he never showed so Tan and I took care of it. I really missed him so I called him and asked if he could come over so we could talk. I planned a special night for us. I hired a chef to come in and cook dinner, I went and got a few sexy pieces from Victoria Secret and even picked up a bottle of D'USSE', his favorite liquor.

He knocked on my door around 10PM and I answered the door wearing barely anything. He walked in the house without saying a word and went straight to the kitchen.

"Ummm hello!" I shouted following behind him.

"What up ma." He responded as he washed his hands in the kitchen sink. "What's for dinner? A nigga hungry as hell."

I stood there looking at him like he had lost his mind.

He acted as if I wasn't standing there as he proceeded to grab two plates out of the cabinet.

"Santiago!" I yelled.

"Why you yelling shorty? I'm right here damn." He said laughing.

I walked over to the stove and bumped him out of the way with my hip, "Go sit down, I will make your plate." I instructed snatching the plate out of his hand.

He laughed "Thanks ma!" he said smacking me on my ass before going to sit at the table.

I could feel his eyes on me as I dished out the food and placed it on two plates. He was still staring as I walked over to the table and placed the plates on the table. I returned to the kitchen to get the bottle and 2 glasses of ice.

"Damn babe, this shit banging!" Santiago said with a mouth full.

"Damn you aint even gonna wait till sit down?" I asked getting increasingly pissed.

"My bad baby, it just smelt so good I had to taste it." He responded laughing again.

I sat the bottle and glasses on the table and sat down at my plate to eat.

"What the fuck is up wit you?" I asked looking him square in the eyes.

"I'm good." He responded.

"You have been real distant lately. I have barely even seen you since I got back from Anguilla." I explained searching for answers.

Santiago shifted in his seat and continued to eat without saying a word.

"Is there something you want to tell me? What's the problem?" I continued to probe.

"Just let it go ok, I said I was good." Was his response.

"Whatever," I threw at him with attitude. "I aint gonna beg you to tell me."

"You really wanna know?" he asked dropping his fork on his plate and wiping his mouth.

"I wouldn't have asked if I didn't" I responded.

"Honestly I don't think the shit is gonna work." He stated.

"What the fuck is that supposed to mean?" I asked.

"You don't have what it takes to be my bitch." He exclaimed.

"WHAT?" I shouted. I was literally 2 seconds for fucking him up, but I kept my cool and let him continue.

"My bitch wouldn't have flown out the country to go lay up with another nigga right after you fucked me, my bitch wouldn't be accepting gifts and shit from anther nigga and my bitch definitely wouldn't have made a move like the other night without me." He continued.

"What are you talkin bout?" I asked puzzled, "What move?"

"That nigga Juice." He responded staring at me.

"That was personal. I couldn't involve too many people." I explained. "How did you know bout it anyway?" I asked.

"You know your cousin got a big ass mouth." He answered.

"Look like I said before, I didn't fuck Angelo, he was barely there the whole time I was there. And the gifts, that's outta my control, it aint like I asked the nigga for anything. I can't help if he like me," I clarified.

"So, you admit that Angelo like you?" he inquired.

"I guess he do, I don't know. Ask him!" I shouted.

"And you feeling him too.... aren't you?" he tested.

I didn't respond I just looked down at my plate of food that was sitting there getting cold.

"Exactly!" he bellowed.

"Naw it aint like that. I mean I aint gonna sit here and lie and say I don't find him attractive. But I don't see myself fuckin with him on that level. I mean he is my MY connect!" I justified.

"Look shorty, it is what it is." He said standing from the table.

"What's that supposed to mean?" I asked.

"Just do you. You are not the first bitch Angelo done swept from under me and you won't be last." He responded.

"You trippin Santiago. You think I would do all this for you if I wanted to fuck with Angelo." I asked.

He looked around the house then at me licking his lips, "Yeah this is cool and all, and you looking sexy as hell in the little that you do have on, but I just aint a nigga that share his bitch." He declared.

"Whatever! I aint gonna keep telling you the same thing over and over. You don't want to fuck wit me no more that's cool. You can leave the same way you came in" I expressed. I was tired of arguing and pleading my case.

"Oh, it's like that." He questioned looking at me with his face screwed up.

"Yep, just like that. I aint interested in begging a nigga to fuck with me." I answered.

"Bet, that's what's up.' He uttered preparing to leave.

He gathered his things and started walking toward the door with me right at his heels.

"Yo and this has nothing to do with business. I expect for you to still do your job." I informed him as I unlocked and opened my front door.

"Oh, you aint got to worry bout that shorty. It's always money over bitches." He sneakered as he walked out my front door. He turned to say something else but before he could get it out I slammed the door in his face.

That nigga got me fucked up. Damn I wish ace had never left I wouldn't be going through this shit.

"I can't believe this bitch had the nerve to slam the door in my face. How the hell she mad at me and she the one living foul?" Santiago asked himself as he started his car to leave Jazzy's house.

"That bitch got me all the way fucked up.... I got something for her though." He said aloud as he took his phone from his pocket and placed a call.

"Hey u!" she said as soon as she answered the phone.

"What's up ma, what you doing?" he asked as if he cared.

"Nothing much laying around thinking bout you." she claimed.

"Oh word? So, does that mean you want a nigga to come over and rub on that booty?" he asked.

"You already know the answer to that." She said laughing.

"Cool I'm on the way. I got some shit I want to talk to you bout anyway." Santiago articulated.

"What is it?" she asked unable to wait.

"I'll explain when I get there. Just know that we bout to take over. You and me, we getting ready to run this shit." He exclaimed.

"You know I'm rockin wit you." Raelynn cried.

"That's what's up baby. I'm on my way." He said before ending the call.

"Dumb bitch" to himself as he made his way to her house.

Unbeknownst to Jazzy, Santiago had been doing his own dirt in her absence. He had been fucking around with her cousin Raelynn, Towns granddaughter. He knew in his heart that Jazzy had fucked Angelo while she was in Anguilla, regardless of what she claimed. This wasn't the first-time Angelo had stolen a chick from him, but unlike the others, he was really feeling Jazzy, so he was hurt. He knew he couldn't compete with Angelo, he was a millionaire and he was Santiago's' boss. Few women would choose the employee over the employer, that's a fact. But he thought Jazzy was different. He felt played, so he formulated a plan to take knock Jazzy off the top and take over. Raelynn held just enough hatred in her heart for Jazzy that he was for sure that she would do anything to help.

CHAPTER 20

I was nervous as I sat at the table after signing in and being searched. I knew my grandma and my Mama was bout to get in my shit. I looked around at all the people waiting to see their loved ones. Being that it is a women's facility, there was mostly men and children. All the children oblivious to what goes on with their loved ones once visiting hours are over.

My Mama and grandma walked in both looking defeated and tired. It hurts my heart to see them like this.

"Hey baby!" my Mama said smiling as they took their seats across from me.

"Hey Mama, Hey grandma." I responded. "How y'all doing?"

"We are good. Just ready to come home." My grandma answered.

"I know, I'm working on it." I returned.

"I heard things are going well for you in the streets." My Mama said proudly.

"Yes ma'am." Was all I could say.

"What's wrong baby? You seem down." My grandma asked.

"I'm ok" I lied. I was still fucked up about all the shit with Santiago and Lil Ray.

"You're lying." My Mama said.

"Mama I don't know what to do about this Ray mess." I admitted.

"What you mean?" my Mama asked with a straight face.

"At the end of the day Ray is a dead man walking." I explained.

"Look baby" my grandma said grabbing my hand, "Ray made the decision to do what he did. He must face his consequences for his actions. We all know that's part of the game, he broke the code." She declared.

"I know grandma but he is fam. Aint nothing I can do?" I asked hopeful.

The women looked at each other then back at me.

"I'm sorry baby but it is what it is." Mama said shaking her head. "It hurts us too, he is my nephew, but he went against the family. He knows how that ends."

"Yeah I know." I said.

"We go to trial in next week, if Ray testifies, we are all looking at 15 to 20 years in here." My grandma relayed. "Sometime you have to cut off a finger to save the hand."

"I have to find him before Angelo does though. Maybe I can get him to leave the country before yall go to court."

"Baby girl, you know I have never been one to sugar coat shit with yall." My Mama said. "It doesn't matter where he goes Angelo will find him and kill him."

"And if he finds out that you helped him he will kill you too." My grandma added.

Her words hit me like a ton of bricks. I could feel the lump in my throat as I tried to fight back tears.

"Don't you sit in here and cry. You had better dry those tears. You know what comes with this game. Sometimes your Judas is closer to you then you think. You have to get rid of anything trying to tear us down, blood or not." My Mama said sternly.

I wiped my face and took a deep breath. I looked around to make sure no one had witnessed my weak moment, luckily for me everyone was engulfed in their own conversations.

"Well," my grandma said changing the subject. "How are your sisters and Tan? Why didn't they come with you?"

"They are good. I will bring them next week." I responded solemnly. It trips me out how they can change the subject like it that.

The rest of the visit went by slowly. I thought my grandma and Mama would give me some sound advice on how to fix this. Apparently, everyone is on the same page and I am in a completely different chapter.

After the visit was over, I rode through the hood just to clear my head. Even though I basically owned this block, I made it my business to stay away. Whenever a situation arose that called for me to come to the block I sent Tan or Santiago. I hadn't stepped foot in the neighborhood since my family got locked up. It was heartbreaking seeing our houses boarded and abandoned as if we never lived there. I felt a tear flow down my cheek as I sat in the car looking at my grandparents' home. I can't believe my own cousin did this shit to us, him, and Juice tore down our kingdom. Now it was up to me to keep our family name respected in the streets. But I couldn't kill my own cousin…. could I?

I drove around Winston for a little while before I headed home. When I pulled in the driveway and noticed that Tan was home, the shit Juice said relayed in my head. It had been eating at me since that night but I hadn't had the chance to talk to Tan about it…until now.

The smell of weed smacked me in the face as soon a son as I walked through the door. I found Tan sitting in the living room watching TV smoking a blunt.

"What up cuz. You came just in time I have something to show you." she stated as I slipped my shoes off and sat on the couch beside her.

She grabbed the remote off the couch beside her and flip to something she recorded on the TiVo.

"This shit been all over the news, I know you don't watch TV so I recorded it for you." she said as she pressed play

"What is it?" I asked

"SHHHH just listen." She responded.

I am here at the Belmont Inn in Clemmons NC where the was discovered by one of the hotel housekeepers. The deceased has been identified as Dewan Burton, a key witness in the Harris Family Trial do to start next week. At the time investigators are do not have any suspects but the motive is very clear. We have reason to believe the without the testimony of Mr. Burton prosecutors do not have a strong case against the Harris Family and could affect the outcome of the trial and the verdict. We will keep you posted as we learn more about this case. This is Laura Bryman reporting live with action live news.

"No suspects" Tan exclaimed.

"Yeah I heard her." I said unenthused.

"What's wrong with you?" she asked.

"Just got a lot of my mind" I responded.

"Where you been all day?" she probed.

"Went to see Mama and grandma then I rode around for a minute to clear my head." I explained.

"Damn why you aint tell nobody you were going, I wanted to see them too." She exclaimed.

"Tan you have a car, you are on their visitation list and you are over 18. You don't need me to go with you to see them, you can go on your own." I said with slight attitude.

"You aint got to get smart." She threw back at me rolling her eyes. "So, what's up with them? Are they alright?" she asked without taking her eyes off the TV.

"Not really." Was my answered.

"What you mean not really?" she quizzed.

"With their trial coming up next week and me still not knowing where Ray is, shit is real tensed." I responded.

"I feel you. So, what you gonna do?" she probed.

"I don't know." I returned shrugging my shoulders.

"I don't know why this is so hard for you." she bellowed.

"What you mean? That's my damn cousin! I don't understand why it's so easy for everybody to brush him off!" I yelled back.

"Because I'm a Harris! That's why." She shouted. "Papa taught all 3 of us he rules to the game. But most importantly he taught us that if somebody don't play by the rules, you take them out of the damn game. Blood or not!"

I just sat there for a minute

"So, since we on the subject, what the fuck was Juice talkin bout the other night?" I asked looking at her with my eyebrow raised.

"I don't know what the hell he was talkin bout." She responded looking away.

"Oh really Tan? What fuckin information is he claiming you gave him?" I figured if I was more direct with my question she may give me a real answer.

"Look Jazzy, it wasn't nothing, just pillow talk." She justified.

"What you mean pillow talk? What the fuck did you tell him?" I barked.

"Look he lied to me! If I would've know he was working for the police I wouldn't have told him shit!" she exclaimed. By this time, she was crying.

"What the fuck did you tell him?" I asked through clenched teeth.

He looked at the floor then back at me "Everything" she said softly.

"Everything?" I repeated loudly.

She just nodded her head as more tears fell from her face.

"Everything like what?" I questioned.

"How the organization is ran, who is who, who does what.... basically everything." She cried.

"Why Tan?" I asked. I could feel the tears forming in my eyes for the third time today.

"He played me. He said he just needed to know how Papa ran his organization without getting knocked so that he could do the same. He said that he was going to take over Towns blocks and I was going to be his first lady." She explained through sobs.

"Yeah he played the fuck outta you. You basically handed him the gun to shoot Papa and Lil Ray supplied the bullets!" I shouted.

"No, it wasn't like that. I thought he really liked me." She wept. "If Papa finds out he's gonna kill me!"

I didn't know whether to hug her or strangle her.

"Stop crying." I said, sliding closer and putting my arm around her. "Don't worry bout it cuz, we gonna keep this between us. That nigga got what he deserved, we will never speak about it again."

She looked at me "I'm sorry cuz. I will never let no nigga get in my head like at again."

"It's all good. I got you." I said.

She burst out laughing.

"What the fuck is so funny?" I asked.

"Girl you should've seen that nigga face in there begging for his life." She responding laughing hysterically.

"What he was saying cuz?" I asked laughing myself.

"Girl he in talking bout... *Please! Please! Don't kill me! I won't testify! I'll get missing, you won't hear from me ever again!*" she laughed imitating him.

She was laughing so hard she could barely talk.

"You crazy you know that?" I chuckled. "I aint fooling with you I'm going to bed." I said standing up and stretching.

"What's going on with you and Santiago, he aint been around lately." She asked.

"Girl that nigga trippin. He accusing me of fuckin Angelo when I was in Anguilla." I disclosed.

"What?" she shouted.

"Yeah girl. He came over here the other day with that shit and I put his ass out." I stated.

"Well did you?" she probed looking at e sideways.

"Bitch you trippin, you know me better than that!" I bellowed.

"Shit I just thought I would ask. I know I would've. That nigga the plug." She exclaimed.

"Yeah we both know you ass would've." I agreed laughing.

"I'm just saying Jazzy, why not? It's obvious that he feeling you." she inquired.

"He is my connect Tan. You know you can't mixed business with pleasure. That shit never ends well." I answered.

"Jazzell be real with me. Deep down you praying that Ace just pop his ass back up don't you?" she prodded.

"In a way, I have put Ace in back of my mind. He didn't care enough about me to even say bye after all we went through." I said.

"I feel you. But you never know. He might be somewhere in the cut, watching yo ass. Waiting on the chance to just pop up." Tan stated.

"Well what the hell is he waiting for, shit if Ace was here we would be running this whole city." I said laughing.

Tan laughed too, "Yeah you right. That nigga is a hustler at heart, this shit is in his blood."

She got quiet for a minute. Then she looked at me and said "We got to find Ray before Angelo does, he is going to kill him."

"Yeah I know" I said sadly.

CHAPTER 21

For the last week, my stomach has been in knots waiting on this day. I have been searching high and low looking for Ray. I had every solider on my team looking for him and still nothing. I didn't want to get Tiffany involved because I didn't want it getting back to Angelo that I was looking for him. Today was the day my family' trial starts and if Ray takes the stand, my family is doomed.

The entire house was silent as we got dressed to head to the courthouse. You could hear a mouse piss on cotton as we walked around as if we were the ones standing trial today. After we got dressed and I dropped my sisters off at school, Tan and I arrived at the courthouse just as the Mayor was giving a statement to the press.

I wasn't interested in shit he had to say so we held hands and climbed the courthouse stairs together, walking straight pass the media circus. We entered the court room and took a seat right in the front. The lawyer came over and spoke with us, assuring us that he was going to do his best to make sure that our family is cleared of all charges. I looked around and noticed that the seats in the court room had filled up quickly, majority were people from the hood that were there to support. It warmed my heart that so many people still had so much love and respect for my family even through these trying times. I noticed that Tiffany was sitting in the back in the corner on her phone. She looked at me and winked. I knew Angelo wouldn't show his face her but I didn't expect him to send Tiffany.

Tan tapped me "Jazzy, there is Papa." She said pointing.

My Papa was escorted into the courtroom in that orange jumpsuit still wearing shackles and handcuffs. Right behind him was my Uncle Troy. He looked over at us and smiled before taking his seat beside his lawyer.

"Please rise!" the bailiff shouted "The court of the Judicial Circuit, Criminal Division, is now in session, the Honorable Judge Stanton presiding" he announced as the judge entered the courtroom and sat on her throne.

Judge Stanton has the reputation as a stern but fair judge. She does not allow any foolishness in her courtroom, so when enter her courtroom, you had better be prepared.

"Good morning ladies and gentlemen. Calling the case of the People of the State of North Carolina verses John Harris. Are both sides ready?

"Ready for the people, Your Honor." The D.A stated.

"Ready for the defense, Your Honor." My Papa's lawyer stated

"Everyone can be seated except for the jury. Bailiff, would you please swear in the jury?" Judge Stanton asked.

After the jury was sworn in and was seated, the D.A gave his opening statement,

"Your Honor and ladies and gentlemen of the jury, the defendant is being charged with felony drug trafficking as well as selling and distributing illegal narcotics. The evidence will show that he along with several members of his family are the leaders of one of the biggest drug organizations in the city. An organization that has flooded our streets with drugs as well as contributed a lot of violent crimes in the community. The evidence presented today will prove to you that the defendant and his family are guilty as charged."

After he was done portraying my family as a gang of monsters. He sat down with a smug look on his face as Papa's lawyer stood to give his opening statement,

"Your Honor and ladies and gentlemen of the jury, under the law my client is innocent until proven guilty. During this trial, you will hear no real evidence against my client. You will come to know the truth about my client John Harris. You will learn that my client is not this vicious drug lord that the people have painted him to be, but in fact a pillar of the community. He has opened business and provided jobs for several people. He donates and host varies charitable events as well as contributed to the election campaign of the Mayor this very city. So, I ask that as the state presents its case please keep in mind that our community will suffer severely if the Harris Family is placed behind bars.

After each side delivered their opening statements the judge said "The prosecution may call its first witness."

"Unfortunately, our two-key witness are unavailable to take the stand." The D.A. announced.

"What do you mean unavailable counselor?" Judge Stanton questioned.

"One as you may have seen in the news was found dead and the other, the defendants' grandson, has gone missing." He responded.

"And the other?" Stanton asked.

"The final witness has recanted their statement." The D.A admitted sounding defeated.

"So, lets me make sure I have a clear understanding, you are trying Mr. Harris on criminal charges and you do not have even 1 of the 3-witness required to indict?" she asked.

"That is correct your Honor. But we do have other evidence, such as the search warrants, photographs and a large amount of money found in the defendants' home with no account of where it originated from." The D.A said reaching.

"That is all circumstantial evidence your Honor," Big Johns' lawyer objected. "My client owns several businesses and does not trust all his money in the bank. That is not a crime."

"Yes, that is correct counselor I read the same law books as you." Judge Stanton replied being smart.

"The defense would like to make a motion for dismissal." Papa's lawyers stated.

"On what grounds?" the D.A shouted.

The judge banged her gravel "There will be order in my court room." she pronounced.

"I apologize your Honor." The D.A retreated.

"The state has had Mr. Harris and his counterparts detained for 6 months. During that time, you have failed to gather enough evidence to indict him let alone keep him detained. Next time you should more prepared when bringing a case into my courtroom. I rule the case be dismissed. Mr. Harris, you are free to go."

The court room erupted.

"Order in the court!" Judge Stanton yelled banging her gavel.

Everyone got quiet.

"Is the same evidence being presented in the cases of the rest of the Harris family." She asked the D.A.

"Yes, your Honor." The D.A answered.

"Well that means my ruling stands for those cases as well." She stated.

I felt like I was going to jump out of my skin, just like that my family was coming home. I thought this was going to be long drawn out process.

"Just a word of advice," Stanton stated pointing her gavel at the D.A, "Do not ever step back into my courtroom without having all your I's dotted and your T's crossed. I will not tolerate the state wasting mine nor the courts time. CASE DISSMISSED!" she reiterated and she bang the gavel once more before rising to leave her bench.

I jumped out of my seat and ran over to my grandfather to finally hug him, I was so overjoyed. As I was hugging him I noticed that Tiffany was slipping through the doors of the court room, still with the phone to her ear.

"I wonder who she talking to?" I thought, but shrugged it off.

As they escorted my Papa and Uncle back to the jail to prepare for their release, I made a few preparations of my own. I called a car service to pick my family members up, I called a maid service to do a good quick clean on my house as well as the chef to prepare an amazing dinner. I also called the school to get me sisters released early so that they will home when everyone walked through the door. My final call was to Angelo.

"Hola Senorita!" he said when he answered.

"Hola Senor! I have some exciting news!" I exclaimed.

"It most certainly can't be more exciting than the release of your family!" he acknowledged.

"How did you know?" I inquired.

"How many times do I have to tell you I know everything?" he affirmed laughing.

"Well I am having a small get together at my house to celebrate and I would love for you to come" I invited.

"Any chance to see that beautiful smile of yours I wouldn't miss for the world." He teased, making me blush.

"Perfect, I will see you around 7." I confirmed before disconnecting the call.

I was on cloud nine. My Papa was a free man!

When my family walked in my house they were all blown away. My Papa could not believe that Ace had built such a luxurious home for me. I had packed all their things from the other houses so everyone had clothes to change into. Once everyone was showered and dressed and Angelo had arrived we sat outside in the backyard, where I had the chef set up dinner for us.

"I'm so proud of you baby girl. You really held this family down." My Papa stated.

"Thanks Papa, but I couldn't have done it without my right hand." I said winking at Tan. She smiled back and continued to eat. She had been very quiet all evening.

"You girls have taken this family to the next level." He continued, "I heard great things while being locked up."

"Well Jazzell definitely is an extraordinary young lady." Angelo added giving me a seductive look that made me uncomfortable. I took a quick glance around the table to see if anyone saw, fortunately for me no one noticed, except Tan. She looked at me and snickered.

"Yes, they both are." My Papa verbalized. He raised his wine glass, "I think they deserve a toast." Everyone followed suit and raised their glasses.

"To my granddaughters, y'all have taken every lesson I have taught yall and made it your own. You two are the reason the Harris name stills holds weight in this town. Yall took over the kingdom and ruled with the style and grace of Queens. We love yall." My Papa spoke.

Everyone cheered and Tan and I couldn't help but grin.

We sat and ate and talked for a little while. As soon as the chef came to serve the dessert Angelo touched Big John on the shoulder.

"Can I speak to you for a minute inside?" he asked.

"Yes, of course." My Papa answered standing up from the table.

Angelo looked at me, "Jazzell would you please join us?"

"Absolutely." I responded.

"Would everyone please excuse us" Angelo said politely to the family, as he stood to leave the table.

The three of us went into the sitting room and closed the door.

"Would either of you gentleman like a drink?" I asked walking over to the bar to pour me a glass of D'USSE'.

"Jazzell, I have only been gone 6 months, I come back and you are drinking? You aren't even old enough." Big John asked astonished.

"A lot has changed a little bit of time." I responded handing both men a drink before sitting down with my own.

Angelo took a sip of his drink and sat down across from me.

"Now that you are home and all that is behind us I wanted to talk to yall about expanding the business." Angelo stated.

"Expanding?" Big John asked.

"Yes, I have already discussed my plans with Jazzell and as a curtesy I felt I should tell you as well." Angelo disclosed.

"Ok well let's hear it." Big John said.

"Well I plan shutting Towns down and taking over his territory. I want the whole city not just half." Angelo announced.

"Ok and how you plan on doing that? Towns and I have an agreement. He stays on his side I stay on mine and everyone lives peacefully. There is enough money out her for everyone to eat." Big John declared.

"Well times have changed. I don't want to share anymore. I want all the money." Angelo stated taking another sip of his drink. "I have someone ready to run that side of town for me. Someone who I know that the both of you will like so there will won't be any beef or rivalry. We're all playing on the same team."

"And who is this person?" Big John asked.

"You know me better than that John, you know I don't show all my cards at one time." Angelo said chuckling.

"Yeah I know." Big John agreed laughing.

"Right now, Jazzell has made a name for herself in the streets, everyone respects her. They fear her just enough that they won't cross her but not too much to where they don't want to work for her. I can say John you groomed those girls well." Angelo complimented smiling at me.

I just smiled and remained silent.

"So, when does all this take place?" Big John asked.

"The election is over in a few days. And because of the outcome of the trial I'm certain that Mayor Taylor will not be re-elected. I plan on making this move after the election is over." Angelo answered.

"That's cool." Big John said nodding his head. "So, Jazzy and I will continue to run our side and this new dude will handle the other side and we can all get this money!" He exclaimed.

Angelo stood up and walked over to the bar to pour him another drink. He then turned and looked at us and said, "That's another thing, I just want Jazzell handling business from now on." He revealed.

"What?" we both said at the same time.

"John, you just got out of jail, you are hot right now. They are watching you. I can't take the chance of having you getting locked up again. It costed me a lot of money to get you and your family home." Angelo proclaimed.

"What you mean, costed you a lot of money?" Big John asked.

"Do you think all he events leading up to this just happened?" Angelo asked. "I paid the last eye witness a visit and we came to an agreement that it was in his best interest not to testify. Judge Stanton and I have had a business relationship for years. Regardless of what the D.A would have presented the Jury would have returned a NOT GUILTY verdict. Fortunately for me, the day I sent someone to go "talk" to that Juice character, someone had already paid him a visit." he revealed looking directly at me.

"So, what do you expect me to do?" Big John questioned.

"Retire, sit back and enjoy the fruits of your labor. Enjoy that beautiful wife of yours. Do whatever you want." Angelo retorted.

"My Papa taught me everything I know about the game. These streets I'm running are his streets, his block. I need him." I stated.

"And you have me!" Big John said looking at me. "Angelo is right it's time for me to retire. I'm always here to make sure nobody fucks with you. But it's time to pass the torch baby."

I looked at them both "Let's get this money!" I exclaimed raising my glass. Both men laughed.

Angelo looked at me and asked "Jazzell have you seen or spoke to Santiago lately?"

I shook my head, "No, he has been moving funny lately. He doesn't even come for the drop offs anymore, he sends Biggs." I informed him.

"What happened to make him change up?" Angelo inquired.

"Things didn't work out between us and he is a little salty about having to report to me." I explained.

"Oh, I see." Angelo said rubbing his neatly trimmed beard.

CHAPTER 22

ACE

I am so ready to get back to the states. Even though I have made A LOT of money here working for Angelo, I miss Jazzy. I sit back and imagine what it will be like when we finally see each other again. It has been so long, I pray that she will understand and forgive me once I explain to her what the really happened. I decided not to tell her about Ray. I mean how would she ever forgive me if she knew I killed her cousin?

Now that Big John is out and the election is almost over I am preparing myself to finally leave Anguilla after being her for 6 months. I will be returning to my city with the 2.5 million I have stacked while I was here as well as the best connect in the game. Once I assemble my team and take Towns down I will be King, finally. I have been grinding and waiting on the moment since I started hustling. Unlike most niggas in the game, my goal was to eventually be the "employer" instead of the "employee". Even though Towns and Big John have had the unspoken agreement, I know Big John is going be happy that his rival is out the game and he and I can run the city together, as partners.

As I was packing my trap phone rang on my night stand.

"Yo" I said answering the phone.

"Acito! How are you my friend?" Angelo's' voice rang through the speaker.

"I'm good Angelo. How are you?" I asked, returning the enthusiasm.

"I am good." He stated, "I need to meet with you today. I need you to come to me home in an hour." Angelo demanded in his deep Spanish accent. He never asked you to do anything, he just told you what you needed to and you had better do it.

"Cool, I will see you then." I responded before ending the call.

I immediately stopped what I was doing and jumped in the shower. After I showered and got dressed I grabbed the duffle bag that was tucked in the back of the closet and was out the door. As my taxi pulled up in front of Angelo's estate, I checked the time on my phone, "Good, I'm early." I said to myself and paid the driver. I exited the car walked up the massive steps to the entrance. Before I could ring the doorbell, Angelo's butler opened the door and I stepped inside.

"Miser Angelo is waiting for you is his office." He stated.

By this time, I had been to Angelo's house so many times that I no longer needed an escort. I nodded and made my way down the long ass hallway. The door was slightly open but I knocked anyway.

"Come in Ace." Angelo said without looking up from whatever he was writing at his desk.

I stepped into his office, closed the door behind me and sat on the leather couch on the other side of the room and waited for Angelo to finish what he was doing. This was something that learned from working for Big John, wait until you are addressed before speaking.

Angelo finished writing and placed some paperwork in his desk drawer.

"Come … Sit" he said waving me over and pointing to the chair sitting directly in front of his desk.

Before I sat down I placed the duffle bag on Angelo's desk.

"Would you like something to drink?" he asked as he picked up his phone and dialed a few numbers.

"Sure, I will take whatever your drinking." I responded nodding at the drink sitting in front of him.

He said something in Spanish to whomever was on the receiving end of his call before hanging up the phone. In a matter of seconds, his butler was coming through the door with a drink for me. He handed me my glass, grabbed the bag off the desk and was out of the room in the blink of an eye.

"Acito, my friend! Life is good yes?" Angelo asked.

"Yes, life is good, it will be even better when I can go home." I stated laughing.

"Indeed, it will." Angelo agreed. "Big John was right about you." he stated.

"Oh yeah?" I asked "How is that?"

"You are a hustler at heart, very loyal, very smart. Very rear for someone so young." He specified.

"Thanks, that means a lot coming from you." I responded.

"The time has come for you to return to the states." Angelo affirmed.

"I know once Big John was released it would only be a matter of time." I said. "But the Mayor hadn't contacted me and said I was good to go back. If I go back too soon, I will be arrested."

"I have handled all that for you my friend." Angelo disclosed.

"Ok" was my response. I couldn't help but think, if he had the power to get my back in the states with no problem, why hadn't he been done it. What was his reason for keeping me here? Angelo was a calculating person, he never did anything without a reason behind it.

"But there are a few things we need to discuss before you leave."
He announced.

"Ok, I'm listening." I said.

"As I have explained to you before, I am shutting Towns entire operation down. But what I neglected to mention is how." He stated. "I want him dead."

"I figured that would be the only way to shut Towns down with the threat of him coming back trying to retaliate." I acknowledged.

"Exactly!" Angelo bellowed. "And the only person I trust to do it is you." he admitted.

"Me?" I asked shocked.

"Si'" was his response.

"What about his connect?" I questioned.

"What about him?" Angelo asked as if he was clueless to what I was asking.

"You don't think that if we murk Towns off that his connect will come looking for us?" I quizzed.

Angelo chuckled, "Oh he will, but I have something in place for that." He informed me.

"Yes, you are always thinking 2 steps ahead." I said laughing with him.

"Ok how soon do you want this handled?' I asked.

"As soon as you touch down. No time to waste." He declared.

"Cool" I said, I always disliked Towns. It would be a pleasure to put a bullet in his head.

"I will have everything set up, all you have to do is go in and do what you do. Just like before." Angelo stated.

The mention of that Ray shit made me uncomfortable, but I kept my cool.

"My associate will call you with the location and time." He continued.

"Bet, I got it." Was all I returned.

"When you return to the city, I need things to go a certain way." Angelo asserted. "I have set it up so that you can run sit but remain low key."

"That's how I move any way." I stated.

"I want my girl Tiffany to be the "Go-To", everyone reports to her she reports to you. She doesn't make a move without you." Angelo instructed.

"Tiffany? Is that the chick from D.R?" I asked.

"Yes, she has been working for me for a long time. She is loyal and can handle herself in the street, but I need you to make sure shit runs smoothly." He instructed.

"Ok, that's cool." I said. "How is Big John? Is he ready for this take over?" I asked.

"My good friend is happy to be home. He is stepping down and retiring from the game." Angelo announced.

"What! Big John retiring? I can't believe it!" I exclaimed.

"Yes, believe it my friend. Cause it's true." Angelo declared laughing.

"That's what's up! So, who is going to take over his block? You know I can handle the whole city. I have worked for Big John for a long time. My name still holds weight on his block." I self-confessed.

"I have someone else in place for that. She has been running his streets the entire time Big John was locked up." Angelo informed.

"She?" I exclaimed shocked. "You got chick running Big John's block? She must be one hell of a hustler."

"Yes, she is one of the best in the game. Taught by the best." Angelo confirmed.

"Who is she? Is she from Winston?" I inquired.

"Now you know I don't expose all my cards in my hand." Angelo said laughing.

"Yeah I know." I responded laughing with him.

"I'm sure the 2 of you will work well together." He confirmed. "So, go home and pack your things, you leave tomorrow morning."

"I'm already packed." I admitted still laughing.

We sat and talked for a little while before I dismissed myself. I had to finish getting myself together to go home. I had waited 6 long months for this and I couldn't wait to touch down.

The next morning I was practically waiting by the door when Angelo's driver arrived to take me to Angelo's private jet. My flight was quick and it felt good to finally be bac in my city. When I finally walked through the door of my apartment I wanted to scream I was so happy to be home. I wanted to pop up on Jazzy, but after thinking long and hard last night, I decided to wait till I took care Towns and got shit situated before I stepped to her. I had waited this long a few more days aint gonna hurt.

I took a shower, rolled my a few blunts and popped opened a bottle of Hennessey. I chilled in the crib and got high and tipsy all day waiting on that call. Around midnight a text message came through my trap phone.

Embassy Suites Downtown
1013
1 hour

I took another shot, put my black hoodie on and walked out the door. When I got to the parking deck of the Embassy Suites downtown Winston-Salem I parked all the way in the corner and waited. I made sure I arrived early to ensure that there would be no surprises.

After about 45 minutes I seen the girl Tiffany come to the door, look around and then propped the door open. After she was gone I exited the car and entered the building. I used the stairs to get to the 10th floor. I had stayed at this hotel several times so I knew the room was right by the emergency exit which was perfect. When I got to the door I noticed that the door wasn't propped open as it was supposed to be. I put my ear to the door hoping I could hear what was going on inside, nothing. I slipped back into the emergency exit stairwell and waited. After a few minutes, she repeated the same routine as the door downstairs. It was time.

I quickly and quietly entered the room. I could hear Towns in the bathroom pissing. I looked at Tiffany motioned for her to leave. She shook her head no and pulled a gun out of her Chanel purse and screwed the silencer in the end of it. I aint gonna lie, that shit turned me on a little bit. When Towns exited the bathroom we both had our guns pointed right at his head.

"What the fuck is this?" he screamed bewildered. "Ace what the fuck are you doing man?" he asked.

I didn't say anything, it was like Tiffany and I could read each other's mind as we started shooting at the same time, emptying our clips into Towns now lifeless body. Tiffany peeped out the door to make sure the coast was clear and we made our exit. Once we got to the parking garage I thought we were gonna go our separate ways but she jumped in my car. I didn't have time to ask any questions, I started the car and sped out of the parking lot.

Once we were on the highway I looked at her and asked, "So where you going?"

"To my place, I live off University Pkwy." She stated.

"Cool" was my simple response.

We rode in silence for a minute and then she said, "So we meet again, too bad it in these circumstance, again. "

"Yeah I guess." I threw back at her.

"Are you ok?" she asked.

"Why wouldn't I be?" I questioned.

"Last time I saw you, you were fucked up behind killing ole boy. I figured he meant something to you. I was just asking." She responded.

"Yeah I'm good. Thanks." I said.

"So, I guess we are going to be seeing a lot of each other from now on." She stated.

"Yeah, and you will quickly learn that I'm not much for small talk and personal conversation. If you handle business and keep your face straight with me, we cool. As you can see I don't give a fuck about brushing anybody off." I declared.

Tiffany busted out laughing, "Obviously, you don't know who the fuck I am! I aint new to this. But you will see." She said through her laughter.

"I guess I will." I said looking over at her. Up until now I hadn't noticed how sexy she is. He swag and her attitude kinda reminded me of Jazzy. I caught myself lusting for a second.

"Make the next left." She said, snatching me out of my thoughts.

"How come I aint never seen you around here before? I know almost everybody in da Tre. You must not be from here." I stated.

"Noticed you said "almost"." She responded. "No personal conversation remember."

"Right." I said nodding my head.

"Make a right at the light and then the first left." She instructed.

I followed her commands even though I know this city like the back of my hand.

"That's my spot right here on the right." She said pointing.

I pulled the car to the curb to let her out. Before she exited the car, I said, "look I think we started off on the wrong foot. We gonna be working closely together, we need to at least be cool."

"You right. We good. I will hit you tomorrow. We got shit to do." She said and got out the car slamming the door behind her. I waited till she was in the house before I pulled off. I wasn't off her street before my phone rang.

"Yo" I said answering the phone.

"Hola my friend." Angelo voice rang through the speaker.

"What's up Angelo." I replied.

"I hear hell has gained a new demon." He stated.

"I heard the same thing." Was my response.

"That's too bad." Angelo lied chuckling.

"Yea." Was all I threw back.

"Tomorrow I am having a gathering at my house. I will send a car for you at 9pm," He announced. "It's a formal affair.

"Ok I will be ready." I agreed.

"Good. It is time for you to meet your partner." He specified.

"Oh, I finally get to meet this infamous Queen that you speak so highly about?" I said laughing.

"Yes, my friend. I am sure you are going to love her. I see the two of running this whole city as partners." Angelo answered laughing as well.

"I hope so. See you tomorrow." I responded before ending the call.

After I hung up my mind drifted back to Tiffany. It is something about her that got me intrigued. No matter what else I tried to think about, she stayed on my mind the rest of the night.

CHAPTER 23

JAZZY

It was Sunday evening, my grandma, Mama, and Aunt Tissie were in the kitchen cooking. My sisters were in their rooms doing their own thing. My Papa and Uncle were in the living room watching football and Tan and I were in the office counting money. We had money everywhere and 3 counting machines going nonstop. It had been a good week on the block and Angelo would be getting more than he expected again this drop.

The doorbell rang unexpectedly and it seemed like the whole house paused. I looked out the window and seen that there was a police car in my driveway.

"Oh shit! Tan, it's the damn police." I bellowed

"What the fuck?" she said frantically trying to put the money away.

"Calm down, if it was anything like that you think they would have only sent one officer?" I stated, smacking my teeth, and heading to the door. "Come on let's see what's going on. Make sure you lock the door." I instructed.

She got up and followed me out of the office, locking the door behind her. By the time we reached the living room, my Uncle had answered the door.

"Good evening officer. How can we help you?' he asked.

"Good evening sir. I hate to bother you this evening, but does Jazzell Harris live here?" he inquired.

"Yes, I'm Jazzell. How can I help you?" I asked approaching the front door.

"This is a very delicate matter, may I come in?" the officer solicited

I looked over at my Papa and he nodded his head, letting me know it was ok to allow the officer to step in.

"Of course," I replied, as my uncle and I step out of the doorway.

"I'm Detective Brennan." He stated as I closed the door after he stepped into the foyer.

"What can we do for you detective?" I asked reiterating my previous question.

"I have been trying to locate the family of Mr. Rayshawn Harris. I have gone to all of their addresses and no one lives at any of them anymore." He declared.

"Yes, I am aware of this. He is my cousin. This is the rest of his family." I announced.

"Oh." Detective Brennan said surprised. "Is his mother here by any chance?" he asked.

By this time the women had come out of the kitchen to see what was going on.

"I'm his mother." My aunt Tissie stated.

He turned and looked at her. There was a weird feeling in the room and a saddened look in his eyes.

"Ma'am I am so sorry to have to tell you this, but your son has been found murdered." He stated.

The room fell silent for a second and then my aunt let out a shriek that made my skin crawl.

"What do you mean? Where? By who?" was the questions coming from each of my family members.

"His body was found in a hotel room in Punta Cana. He was shot in the head." Detective Brennan informed.

"Punta Cana? …. The Dominican Republic? What the hell was he doing there?" my Papa asked.

"I'm not sure sir. From the report, there was an excessive amount of cocaine in the room as well as in his system, so my guess it had something to do with drugs." Brennan answered.

"Where is his body now?" my grandmother cried.

"It is at the city morgue. It was shipped back to the states 2 days ago," he stated. "I am so sorry for your loss. Unfortunately, being that this unspeakable act happened outside of the country, the authorities in Punta Cana will be investigating the case. We will keep the family updated as we get news." He explained.

The room was filled with sobs and sniffles. I felt as if I was going to faint. I can't believe my cousin is dead.

"We need someone to come down and identify the body today." Brennan announced.

"Yes sir. Someone will be there right away. Thank you." my uncle said, he seemed to be the only one holding it together.

"Again, I am sorry for your loss. We will let you know if we find out anything." He replied before leaving.

Once he was gone and the door was closed, my aunt lost it.

"What have you done?" she yelled at my Papa. "I know you did this!"

My Papa jumped up, "I had nothing to do with this."

"LIAR!" she screamed, "He's your fucking grandson! What have you done?"

"John," my grandma said calmly while holding my aunt "Did you do this?" she asked.

"NO!" he yelled tears pouring down his face.

My aunt, who was now on the floor was crying hysterically.

My Papa looked around the room at each of us, "I have always been an honest man, I have never lied to any of you." he said through sobs. "I had nothing to do with Lil Ray getting killed!"

I looked my Papa in the eyes and knew immediately that he was telling the truth.

"I believe you Papa." Tan said from the corner she had been standing in.

"Me too." I added.

"Well who did this then?" my aunt cried.

"Baby, I promise I will do everything in my power to find out." My Papa promised and he left the room.

I just sat there, numb. I knew that eventually it was going to happen after what he did. But secretly I prayed that my cousin was smart enough to get missing and never come back. I could have taken never seeing him again a lot better than the news of him being murdered.

"I'm gonna go do and identify his body so we can start making arrangements" my Uncle Troy said, still calm.

"I'm going with you." my sister Cyn announced. Everyone turned and looked at her like she was crazy.

"Are you sure you can handle that baby girl?" my uncle questioned.

"Yes sir." She answered.

Up until now I hadn't noticed that she was the only one besides my Uncle Troy that was unbothered by the news. Not one tear, no emotion, she doesn't even seem surprised.

"I'm going too." I said, never taking my eyes off Cyn. She looked back at me and gave me a smirk before going upstairs to prepare to leave.

"What the fuck was that about?" Tan came over and whispered to me.

"Oh you peeped that shit too?" I asked.

"MmmmHmmm." She responded.

"Oh, I'm going to get to the bottom of it. Believe that." I declared. "But now ain't the time."

We drove to the morgue in silence. Once we got there we were escorted to a large glass window. One of workers rolled a table in front of window that had a white sheet covering its contents. She pulled the sheet back, and there he was, my cousin, laying on that cold metal table with a hole in his head.

Tears instantly stung my eyes and blurred my vison. I looked up at my Uncle, his face soaked with tears. I knew it was coming, he didn't want to break down in front of my aunt. I then looked at me sister, and she was just starring at the body with a smirk on her face.

"What the fuck is wrong with you?" I questioned.

She looked at me and screwed her face up.

"Who you talking to?" she asked.

"You!" I yelled. "Your cousin is dead and you sitting here wit a smirk on your face. What the fuck is wrong with you?"

"Yall calm down this is not the time nor place for this." Uncle Troy intervened

Cyn walked closer to me, right in my face and said through clinched teeth, "He got what he deserved." And she walked off leaving both my uncle and I standing there shocked.

"Let's go Jazzy." My Uncle said putting his arm around my shoulders, leading me to the exit.

Cyn was leaning on the car talking on her phone when we walked outside.

"Cynthia hang up the phone and get yo ass in the car!" I said as my Uncle unlocked the car doors.

She looked at me, rolled her eyes, and kept talking.

Before I knew it, I was in her face, "Did you hear what the hell I said!"

"I'll call you back." She said to whoever she was on the phone with and disconnected the call. She folded her arms and looked at me.

"WHAT!" she yelled.

"Who in the hell are you talking to? You'd better watch yo damn mouth!" I hollered back.

"Yo you aint my Mama!" she yelled back.

"No but I will still beat the shit outta yo disrespectful ass out her. How dare you stand there drippin in all the shit I done bought, and talk shit? What the fuck is yo problem?" I barked.

"Yall phony as hell. I can't stand this damn family." She hollered.

"What the fuck you talkin bout girl?" my uncle yelled, he had had enough.

"Just last week yall was talking bout killing Ray so that he wouldn't testify, now yall sitting around crying cause he dead." She explained. "Which one is it? My uncle Troy and I looked at each other, neither able to respond.

"He was a snitch, he was trying to destroy our family. If you ask me, whoever killed him did yall a favor." She shrugged.

I looked at her, "Look I said calmly. "Yes, Ray crossed the line, and yes we were looking for him. but nobody was gonna kill him. He's family."

She looked me square in the eye, "Yall must think I'm stupid. I grew up in the same house as you Jazzy.

Just because I don't say nothing don't mean I don't hear shit. Papa was going to kill Ray when yall found him, that's facts. And I don't blame him. Hustlers and snitches can't co-exist in the same circle." Cyn bellowed and got in the car, slamming the door.

I couldn't say anything, uncle Troy couldn't say anything, she was right. The ride back to the house the same way we rode there, in silence.

As soon as I stepped back in the house, I went straight to my office and closed the door. I needed a few minutes to myself. As I noticed Tan had finished counting the money and had it all bagged up and ready to be delivered. I sat in the chair at my desk and put my head down, then my phone rang.

"Hello" I answered with attitude.

"Hola Senorita." Angelo sang into the phone.

"Hola Angelo." I responded dryly

"I'm so sorry for your loss. I heard about your cousin." Angelo announced.

I took the phone from my ear and looked at it shocked.

"How'd you know so soon. We just found out." I tested.

"You already know my answer to that Jazzel, it amazing me how you seem to keep forgetting." He responded.

"Yeah, you know everything." I sang unenthused.

"Is there anything the family needs, is everyone holding up ok?" he asked.

"We're gonna be all right. It's just gonna take some time. But we gotta keep pushing. This money aint gone make itself." I said.

"That's my girl. With I am having a gathering at my estate tomorrow evening, formal attire please." I will send a car to get you guys at 9am." He proclaimed.

"Of course, I will let my Papa know." I replied.

"I need Tan to come as well." He added.

"Tan?" I asked astonished.

"Yes, Tan. I have some announcements as well as I will be introducing yall to the member of this organization." He clarified.

"Oh, we finally get to meet your Ace in the Hole!" I said chuckling.

"You have no idea how befitting your choice of words truly are." he replied laughing as well.

"Ok see you then." I said and he disconnected the call.

CHAPTER 24

Santiago and Raelynn were knocked out sleep after their intense fucking session when her phone kept ringing non-stop.

"Aye yo you gonna get that?" Santiago asked nudging Raelynn.

She moaned and rolled over to grab her phone off the nightstand.

"Hello" she said answering it without looking at the caller ID. She swung her feet off the bed and went to the bathroom to take the call so she wouldn't disturb Santiago who had went back to sleep.

His rest didn't last long because he was awaken by Raelyn screaming and crying. He jumped up and ran to the bathroom door.

"Rae are you ok? He asked knocking on the door.

She didn't respond, all he heard was her crying and sobbing. He opened the door and peeked in, she was sitting on the floor Indian style with her face in her hands crying hysterically.

"What happened? What's going on?" Santiago asked putting the lid down and sitting on the toilet.

She looked up at him with her tear soaked face, "He's dead." She cried.

"Who?" he asked confused.

"My grandfather. They found him in a hotel room shot up." She explained.

"What!" Santiago shouted.

Raelyn broke down crying again, "Who could've done this?" she said through her sobs.

"Come on get off the floor." He said lifting her up and carrying her to the bed. Just as he was about to lay down beside her his phone started ringing.

"Yo" he answered after digging it out him pants pocket.

"Hola Amigo. It's been a long time my friend." Angelo sang in the phone.

"Yo what up Angelo." Santiago smirked.

"I haven't heard from you. Where have you been?" Angelo asked.

"I've been busy, getting this money. Keeping you rich." Santiago said with attitude.

"Interesting." Angelo retorted.

"So what's up?" Santiago asked impatiently.

"I am having a meeting to announce some changes in the organization. I will be sending a car for you at 9:30pm." Angelo disclosed.

"Why do I need to be there? Jazzy's in charge, right? She can relate anything to me when she tells the other soldiers." Santiago barked.

"So, you expect me to repeat myself?" Angelo asked calmly.

"I'll be there." Santiago roared.

"It is a formal affair, so I need you to dress appropriately." Angelo informed him.

"I will be casket sharp" Santiago said laughing sarcastically.

"My sentiments exactly." Angelo replied before hanging up the phone.

By this time, Raelyn was sitting up on the side of the bad. Her mood had shifted from sad to angry.

"I got to find out who did this." She said staring at the floor.

Santiago came over and sat on the bed beside her.

"I'm gonna be all the way real wit you shorty. You grandfather had a lot of secret enemies. This could've been anybody." He expressed.

"What you mean secret enemies? She snapped.

"Look don't get mad at me. Let's face it Town was not the easiest person to work for. Any of his workers could've gotten fed up and killed him" Santiago stated.

"Naw I got a feeling it's something else to this. And I'm gonna find out who is behind this." She said.

"You worried about the wrong shit. You need to be trying to hit his connect up so you can continue to run his streets and keep his legacy going." Santiago declared.

"I guess you're right." Raelyn uttered.

"But I will ask around and see if anybody heard or seen anything." He spoke. "Who called you and told you he was dead?"

"My friend Tonya. She said it's been all over the news all morning." she answered.

"Did she say anything else?" Santiago probed.

"No." she answered shaking her head.

"He was all I had Santiago. What am I gonna do without him?" she sobbed.

"I got you baby girl. You got me." He said hugging her. "And I'm going to help you boss up. When you getting money, you don't need no damn family. Trust me I know." He stated reflecting on his own fucked up family "Come on let's get dressed and ride out. We need to go do some digging, ask some questions, see what we come up with."

"Ok" she spoke softly.

While she was in the shower he could hear her crying softly. He kinda felt sorry for her for a second. But his mission to get back a Jazzy and Angelo was far too important to be distracted now.

Towns being dead was a good thing for Santiago. Shit, whoever killed him did him a favor, it saved him from having to do it himself. Now he can get from up under Angelo and Jazzy's thumb and run his own shit. He just needed Raelyn to get in touch with whomever Town's connect is so they can take over his side.

Santiago had been playing both sides of the fence for years now. Being that he had known Towns since he was a kid gave him an advantage on Towns side of town. He had worked for Towns for a little, but he hated the way Towns treats his people. When his ex-girlfriend introduced him to Angelo, he started working for him on the low but was still fucking with Towns.

Santiago was known in the hood for his "don't give a fuck" attitude. He would put a bullet in anybody head, didn't matter who. If you cross him or for the right price, he would make you disappear. His family didn't fuck with him because they believed he had something to do with the murder of his uncle, it was never proven. On top of that he was a hell of a hustler, he knew the game forwards and backward. And therefore, Towns and Angelo both, unbeknownst to them, kept him on their team.

He and Angelo became closer when he overheard his ex-girlfriend plotting to rob Angelo. Instead of reporting it straight to Angelo, he confronted her about it, and convinced her to let him be included. On the day, it all went down, everything went per plan, except Santiago had his own agenda. He ended up killing his girl and her friend and delivered the money back to Angelo. Angelo had been promising his own shit since then. But instead he put Jazzy on and made Santiago her right hand. Santiago was cool with it at first, Jazzy caught on quick, she knew how to get that money. Plus, he was really feeling her. But when they played him and started fucking behind his back all that changed. It was time for him to run shit. He had gone from working from Towns, to working for Angelo and now working for Jazzy. His time as an employee was over. Fortunately, Raelyn was just the right dummy to help him do just that. He was gonna pretend like he cared, just to get ahold of Towns connect. Then he would take over and get rid of her ass. The fact she was Jazzy's cousin was a bonus.

They got dressed and went straight to Easton, Towns block. The hood looked deserted, it was obvious the news of Towns death had spread. The first person they ran into was Lil Red, one of Towns soldiers. He claimed he hadn't seen nor heard from Towns in a couple of days.

"He had started fucking wit some chick that had his mind gone." Lil Red, stated. "He wasn't coming around no more, he didn't even Re-UP with the connect. So, the connect never got his money and we hadn't gotten in new shit in a few days. We bout out."

"So, who is this chick, where she from?" Raelyn asked Red.

"Hell if I know. He didn't bring her around." Was his response.

"Where is everybody?" She asked looking around.

"With Towns gone aint nobody got no work. Its drying up out here. Niggas talking bout going to the east side to holla at Jazzy."

The sound of Jazzy's name made Santiago's blood boil.

"Yall just be patient, we got yall." Santiago said to Lil Red.

"Yall got us?" Lil Red questioned looking at them both. "Oh ok." He snickered.

"Real talk we got yall. Give me a few days." Santiago reiterated.

"Aight we'll see. I will give yall a couple days." he said "Once the rest of this pack I got now is gone and yall aint came through, I'm going to holla at ole girl." He looked at Raelyn with sympathy, "I'm sorry for your loss baby girl, but shit don't stop. I got a family to feed."

"I can't do nothing but respect it." She replied. "You know I got you though. Just give me a few days to get right."

"Bet." He responded nodding his head.

On the way to the car Santiago said, "See the streets need us. If we don't get in touch wit Towns plug Jazzy gonna eventually have this whole shit on lock. We can't afford that. Is that what you want?"

"Hell no! Aint no way I'm going to let that bitch move in on my Grandfather's shit. Let's get this shit poppin." She exclaimed.

"Let's do it then." Santiago said excited. All the pieces to his plan was falling together.

"I have to go down to the morgue and ID his body. Can you go with me?" she begged as Santiago opened the passenger side door for her to slid in.

"I got you shorty." He responded before he slammed the door and climbed in the drivers' seat.

Even though he was not too much older than her, Santiago had watched Raelyn grow up. He knew that her Grandma died when she was very young and that Towns only had 2 sons. His oldest, Calvin, which was Jazzy's father was killed by a local drug dealer after he tried to rob him. His youngster son Ray, Raelyn's' father, was killed by her mother, who is now serving a life sentence in prison. Towns took care of Raelyn, gave her everything she could ever want. But he also kept her sheltered, so she was naïve to a lot of things. What she did know about the game, which wasn't much, she learned from niggas she dated.

They made their way out of the hood and headed for the morgue in downtown Winston.

"My grandfathers' connect is my god-father, his name is Terrio." She stated out the blue.

"Terrio?" Santiago probed. "I have never heard of him. He from Winston?" he quizzed.

"Naw he lives in South Carolina, by the beach. That's where my grandfather is originally from, they grew up together." She explained.

"Do you know how to get in touch with him?" he inquired.

She nodded her head yes.

"You gonna have to call him when we get back to the house." He asserted.

"Dam I still have to make funeral arrangement and shit for my grandfather. He did just die. Can I get through that first?" Raelyn snapped tears rolling down her cheek.

"This shit can't wait Raelyn! Yo ass be stuck somewhere broke and looking stupid. The game doesn't stop for nobody. Aint no sick and bereavement days." Santiago yelled. "You gotta strike while the iron is hot."

She looked down and continued to cry.

"Look I'm sorry for yelling." He said lowering his voice. "I just don't want you to let your grandfathers' legacy just die like that. He is gone baby, you have nobody else to depend on but you. You've got to boss up."

"You're right." She admitted. "I will call him as soon as we get back to my crib. I need your help with this though. I don't know shit about the game."

"I got you baby. You get the product I can show you how to move it." He returned.

"Thanks Santiago. I'm glad you're in my corner. You're all I got right now." She declared.

"You can trust me." Santiago avowed.

CHAPTER 25

ACE

I took a shower and went to bed as soon as soon as I got home. I couldn't sleep so I just laid there looking at the ceiling. I can't wait to see Jazzy's face. To touch her and kiss her. I hope that she understands why I did what I did, especially after she sees the moves I have made for her us.

After this meeting tomorrow and the official takeover of Towns territory, I will be the king of the city. I will be able to step back into Jazzy's life and pick up where we left off, only my pockets are gonna be a lot fatter. I trust Angelo, but I don't plan on being partners with no one for long. I am going to go along with his plan until I get my team in place and shit running the way I want it to run. Then I'm going to get rid of whoever this new chick is. I was born and raised in City View, that's is my hood, those are my streets! I have put so much blood, sweat and tears into that block, I'll be damn if I let anybody run it but me. I don't give a damn wo it is. Even Big John himself couldn't stop me from taking over that block. I am shutting anybody down that stands in my way of being King of da Tre, finally.

I finally drifted off to sleep around 3am but was right back up at 9am. I had a busy day ahead of me. I got a lot to do, but I must stay low key. I don't want to risk the chance of running into Jazzy or Tan anywhere. No one knew I was back in town except for Tiffany and Angelo, and I wanted to keep it that way.

First things first I had to go get me a new suit. Instead of going to the mall in Winston, I decided to drive the hour away to Charlotte and make a day of it. I got my dreds twisted, got a fresh line up, even treated myself to dinner at infamous Firebirds Restaurant. After getting my Tom Ford suit tailored for the perfect fit, I grabbed me a pair of Saint Laurent loafers out of Neiman Marcus and was back on 85 south by 5 o'clock.

When I got back to the Tre, I decided to do a ride through of what was getting ready to be "my hood." I took note of who the corner boys were, where the lookouts were placed, and how the whole operation was ran overall. I didn't know if it was because Towns was no longer there, but this whole set up was sloppy as hell. These boys trying to get knocked.

I was sitting back in the cut when I noticed a dude I went to school with.

I rolled my window down "Aye yo Red come here man." I yelled at him.

"He stopped and looked as if he didn't recognize me, so I stepped out of the car.

"Oh, shit dat nigga Ace." He laughed as he jogged over to me. "Yo what up fam." He greeted when he finally reached my car.

"Yo what's good?" I asked dapping him up.

"Shit, you already know. Getting this money. What you doing over here? This aint even yo neck of the woods?" he quizzed.

"Not yet, but that's bout to change real soon." I replied. "Who the hell running this shit? yall just doin what the fuck yall want to do out here."

"Pretty much. Ever since Towns got merked, niggas been out here wildin. Most of these fools can't function without a boss. Everybody doing their own thing." He stated.

"I see." Was my response. "Yo, I want you to work for me."

"Nigga where on O.G.B? ... You know those City View niggas aint bout to let me come make no dough over there." He declared.

"Naw, I got some other shit in the works." I assured him.

"Oh word. Well anything is better than this nickel and dime bullshit out here." Red conceded.

"I'll tell you what. Gather up your best soldiers. The ones that you know is hungry and ready to make this money and yall meet me Forsyth Seafood on MLK Blvd tomorrow afternoon around 1." I instructed.

"Cool. We will be there." Lil Red confirmed.

"Aight bet! I'll holla you tomorrow." I said as I dapped him up before leaving.

"Damn this shit gonna easier than I thought?" I said aloud.

Once I got home I poured me a glass of some Pure White Hennessy that I brought back from Anguilla, rolled me a blunt of some loud, also curtsey of Anguilla, and took a shower. I had to get in my zone, tonight was a big night. By the time the driver knocked on my door I looked and felt like money.

When the driver open the back door to the Lincoln Town car, I immediately caught the whiff of sweet perfume. I noticed a sexy caramel leg poking out of a spilt that stop and started at the thigh. It was dressed with the sexiest pair of Giuseppe pumps. I slid in the car beside her and the door was shut behind me. The smile she gave made my dick jump in my pants.

"Buena noches, Senor Ace." She said through her pearly white teeth.

"Good evening Tiffany." I replied, "You look amazing."

"Gracias" she said smiling and handed me a glass champagne. It wasn't until then I noticed the ice bucket with a bottle of Ace of Spades sitting on the floor in between us.

"So, you speak Spanish now?" I asked laughing.

She laughed, "You are funny you know that."

"So, what are you, Dominican, Brazilian?" I probed, it was hard to tell.

"A little bit of everything." Was her answer as she sipped her champagne.

"Oh wow! We secretive now." I tested, still chuckling.

"You're the one that said no small talk and no personal conversation." She smirked.

I nodded my head, "Indeed I did." I replied.

"But since we have such a long ride, we may as well get to know each other. Since we are going to working so closely." She said seductively.

"A long ride? Where we going?" I questioned.

"To Angelo's estate, its bout an hour and a half ride." She answered.

"Oh, that's not bad." I replied.

"Yes, just enough time." She added.

"Just enough time for what?" I asked.

"It's long enough for me to know a little more about you, not too long where it takes away the mystery." She sang.

"Hmmmm interesting." I replied grinning.

Jazzy

I stood in the mirror looking at myself. "DAMN I'M BAD" I shouted to myself. I had chosen a sexy pants suit instead of a dress. I thought it was perfect for the occasion. I wore my impeccably tailored black Tom Ford suit as if it was a second skin. My breast sat up succulently under the deep cut in the jacket as the diamond key necklace that Ace had given me lay flawlessly in between.

My pants laid effortlessly on my Yves Saint Laurent strappy sandals that matched my YSL clutch. I wore my hair straight back, showing off my flawlessly made up face that accented my exquisite features. I added another coat of MAC lip gloss, dowsed myself in my favorite Miss Dior Perfume and headed downstairs.

"Damn my babies are all grown up!" my Papa said looking at my cousin and I smiling.

Tan was standing in the kitchen pouring 3 glasses of champagne. She was looked like she just stepped out Vogue Magazine, she was so beautiful. Her dress was gold sequins and long. It hugged every curve on her body as it stopped just at the floor. She looked elegant with her hair pinned up and off her face. Showing her true African features. She reminded me of the African Princess from the movie Coming to America.

My grandfather was looking like himself again. His twinkle in his eyes was back and he had a permanent smile plastered on his face lately. He looked handsome in his Armani suit that fit him like a glove.

At exactly 9pm the driver rang the doorbell. I instructed the driver to grab the 2 duffle bags off the floor and place them in the trunk of the limo.

"What's that?" Big John.

"You taught us to never show up at a party empty handed." Tan laughed.

"That's Angelo's cut for the week." I said shaking my head and laughing.

"Damn baby girl, yall pulling in numbers like that?" he asked astonished.

"You'd better know it!" said proudly as we walked out the door to climb into the limo.

As soon as we got in and the doors were closed behind us, my grandfather leaned over to me and said, "If yall can pull in numbers like that in a week from only our side, imagine what yall can make if we had the whole city."

"I was thinking the same thing Papa." Tan disclosed, popping open the bottle of Ace of Spades that was in the ice bucket in the seat beside her. She poured each of us a glass before asking, "Who the hell is this new dude anyway? Where he come from?"

"I don't know Angelo said we will meet him tonight. I do know that he rocking with that chick Tiffany" I responded.

"Oh word, Tiffany cool, but I still don't know that bitch like that. I don't know about working with someone we don't know." Tan stated shaking her head.

"Yes, I have thought about that a lot too. I don't mind working with Tiffany, she a rider, especially after the shit she done helped us with." I disclosed, "But I know Angelo, he aint gonna put somebody in this shit who he aint fully checked out." I explained.

"Yeah you right Jazzy, but this is our city. I made a truce with Towns back in the day because too many people were getting killed behind our beef. But now that Towns is gone, that territory is rightfully ours." Big John explained.

"Technically it is ours if we are partners with whoever Angelo put in place to run it." I defended.

"Fuck technical, we ant gonna see no money from it. So I don't understand this partner bullshit." Tan barked. "The point is so Angelo can get richer cause he will the plug for the entire city. We not benefiting nothing"

"Your cousin has a point baby." Papa agreed.

"So, what are yall suggesting we do then? We can't go against Angelo. Then we will be fucked, with no connect." I tested.

"I say we dry this new nigga out and have Tiffany come work with us." Tan announced.

"Dry him out?" I asked.

"Yes, this is our city. We know everybody. Our face is good on any side of town. We can just make it so people would rather Re-Up with us instead of him, recruit all his good soldiers so that he don't have a team. Once Angelo see's he aint making no money and can't handle his squad he gonna brush him. Then the city will be ours." Tan explained her plan.

I didn't say anything, I just nodded and listened.

"Baby girl when I first started hustling, I was a corner boy just like Ray and Ace. But I knew that wasn't the spot for me. I wanted more. I was working for a dude named Terrio. He was from out of town and he had the city on lock. After putting in years of work I went to him and asked him for a promotion, and do you know what he told me?" My Papa asked.

"What?" tan and I said at the same time, engulfed in his story.

"He said nothing in the game is given to you, you have to let your balls drop and take it." He replied.

"So, what you do?" Tan probed for more.

"I found me a new connect with better shit, recruited some solders, and I took over his block. We didn't let any of his workers make a dime on the streets. We were ruthless, anybody got caught slipping got fucked up every time, until they got the point. Most of his people ended up working form me while the others either went to work for Towns or the didn't make it." Big John revealed.

"So, what happened to the Terrio dude?" I questioned.

"Last I heard he was back in his hometown in South Carolina. They say he moving big weight out there but he never came back to the city." Big John answered.

"See that's what I'm talking bout Jazzy, we gonna have to get on or New Jack City shit, either you get down or you lay down." She exclaimed excited.

My Papa and I both laughed.

"Yo ass is crazy you know that." I chuckled.

The rest of the ride I sat drinking, looking out the window, and thinking. Maybe my family is right, I mean these are our streets. We have Tre-4 pumping through our blood. How could we let some new nigga come in and run our streets? After all the work, I have put in for Angelo while my Papa was locked up, I made him a lot of money. I feel boarder line disrespected that he even thought it was cool to move some random nigga in. What part of the game was that?

I made the decision, I want the whole city, I don't want to share. I want I all, and I'm going to take it.

SANTIAGO

After we left the morgue we got back to her house. She bullshitted around about calling Terrio, so I had to give her a little incentive. After fucking her good and making her cum back to back she was willing and ready to do whatever I needed her to do. Unfortunately, it didn't go completely as planned.

Terrio, like any other nigga in the game was skeptically bout fucking with me right away, because he didn't know me. I was ready to give up, I mean I wasn't bout to beg a nigga to fuck with me, until Raelyn got him to agree to meet me. we arranged to come to South Carolina tomorrow morning for a sit down. If the nigga aint acting right, I'm just gonna rob his ass, either way I'm coming home with some work.

I went back and forth with myself whether to take Raelyn to this meeting with me. I know it's gonna blow Jazzy's mind to see me walk in with her cousin on my arm. So, I decided to take the petty route and take her along.

I had to get her mind off her grandfathers' death so she could focus, so I took her shopping. We spent the whole day in and out of stores before we retired at my house for the evening. I usually don't let chicks come to my crib, but I had to make this shit believable.

The next day I sent her to get her hair and nails done while I enjoyed some peace and quiet. I had to get my mind right for this meeting. When she returned, she went and took a bubble bath in the guest room while I showered in my bathroom. I didn't realize how gorgeous she is until she walked out of the room full dressed and ready to go. She picked out a red long strapless evening gown with a split the that reached the top of her pelvic without showing too much. I have a fetish for long curly hair and hers was perfect in the ringlets her stylist framed her face with. Her small size 5 feet were jeweled in a sliver pair of Jimmy Choo strappy sandals that made her toes look suck able.

"Damn!" I let slip out as I looked at her from head to toe.

She looked at me and smiled. "You like baby?" she asked doing a spin in front of me.

"Hell yeah, you look beautiful." I confessed.

"Thank you. You are looking quite sexy yourself." She replied. And leaned in to kiss me.

Just as our lips touched there was a knock at the door.

I grabbed my gun off the counter and looked through the peephole.

"Oh, it's the driver." I stated unlocking the door.

"Ok let me grab my purse." she threw over her shoulder as she skipped to the guest room.

Once we were in the car and on our way, I popped the bottle of Ace of Spades open that was resting in an ice bucket on the floor of the car. I filled two glasses and handed her one. It never crossed my mind as to why there where 2 glasses in the car when Angelo was expecting me.

"Let's toast to the tonight!" Raelyn said raising her glass for a toast.

"No, to the takeover!" I corrected as we clanked glasses.

She took a sip and then asked, "So where are we going?"

"I have business meeting with a soon to be ex associate." I replied.

"Oh ok. So why did you need me to come." She quizzed.

"To make a statement. You don't even have to do nothing, just sit back, and look beautiful. This is your introduction to the game baby." I stated, boosting her head up.

It worked because she was grinning from ear to ear. I just hope she can keep that composure when she walks in and see Jazzy.

THE MEETING

Each driver was instructed to pull into a different entrance to Angelo's estate. Santiago came through the back entrance and was seated in the formal dining room at the table. Ace and Tiffany was lead through the side door and was asked to wait in Angelo's office. While Jazzel, Tan and Big John were escorted through the front entrance to one of the 3 living rooms.

"Santiago! My friend. Welcome to my estate." Angelo exclaimed as he entered the dining room with his arms stretched out. "And who is this enchanting young lady?" he asked looking at Raelyn.

Santiago and Raelyn remained seated.

"This my girl Rae, Rae this Angelo." Santiago said with an attitude.

"Santiago, it is both customary and polite to stand a greet someone when they enter the room." Angelo replied.

"Yo fuck all that. Where is everybody at?" Santiago snarled grilling Angelo.

"YO! You watch your tone in my house!" Angelo yelled making Raelyn jump.

The two men sat there grilling each other for a few seconds,

"My bad Angelo." Santiago uttered dropping his head.

Raelyn had never seen Santiago back down from anyone. She just sat there quiet.

"That's better." Angelo stated straighten his suit jacket. "Can you please escort my guest in the living room in?" he instructed the butler who was standing by the door.

The butler nodded and proceeded to the living room.

"Senor Angelo is ready for you, right this way." He announced.

Tan, Jazzy and John followed as he led them to the dining room. As soon Jazzy and Raelyn locked eyes both ladies' mouths dropped.

"Welcome." Angelo's face lit up when he seen Jazzy.

She broke her glare at Raelyn and smiled at Angelo.

"Thank you for having us, it's always a pleasure to be a guest in your beautiful home." She said hugging him.

Tan and Big John copied the gestured before seating at the table.

"*What the fuck is she doing here?*" Jazzy thought to herself, "*and with Santiago.*"

She was so busy glaring at Tonya she didn't pay attention to Santiago glaring at her. But Big John and Tan were on it.

"So much tension in the room." Angelo stated. "Santiago, aren't you happy to see Jazzel?" he asked chuckling.

"Can we just get on with this meeting I got to get back to the money." He responded never taking his eyes off Jazzy.

"Mmmmhmm. Let's just make sure your drop not late next time." Tan stated chuckling.

He shot Tan the evil eye and snickered.

"So, I have brought you all together to announce a few changes we are making to the organization." Angelo started.

"Wait a minute! Hold up!" Jazzel cut him off, "Are we really bout to talk bout this with her in the room?" she asked pointing at Raelyn.

"Yes! Raelyn is my new partner, my new right hand." Santiago informed.

"Your new partner? Since when? Last time I checked employees didn't have the authority to hire." Jazzy gnarled.

"Employee?" Raelyn asked looking at Santiago. "What do she mean employee?"

"Oh, you didn't know this nigga work for me?" Jazzy tested laughing, "Next time do more research on the nigga you fuckin!"

Raelyn didn't respond, she sat there with her mouth screwed up.

"Like I was saying." Jazzy continued looking at Angelo. "Do you know who she is?"

"Who is she?" Tan asked.

"She does look familiar." Big John stated rubbing his beard. Then it hit him. "That's Towns granddaughter." He exclaimed.

Angelo and Tan both looked shocked.

"What the fuck?" Tan said in a hushed tone.

"I am surprised by very little and this baffles me. I knew you had a new lady in your life ... I even knew you was bringing her tonight, hence the 2-champagne glass in your car and the table set-up with a seat for her. But I didn't know this. I don't how this got passed me." Angelo stated.

"Humph...I guess you don't everything like you thought you do." Santiago uttered.

"Indeed.... Senorita?" Angelo said looking at Raelyn, "Is Towns your grandfather?"

"Yes" she replied.

"Do you realize you are in a room full of his competitors?" Angelo probed looking confused.

"No I didn't know that." She said glaring at Santiago while everyone stared at her.

"Interesting." Angelo nodding his head. "But Santiago knew and yet he still brought you here."

Santiago showed no shame, no worries, he sat there with his chest poked out, no emotion on his face, not saying a word.

"Well what an intriguing turn of events." Angelo continued, as he walked around the table. "And it's getting ready to get better."

"Senorita Raelyn, let me apologize on behalf of my absent-minded friend. I'm sure he didn't intend on putting you in such a compromising position." He said stopping behind me a putting his hands on my shoulders.

Jazzy continued to glare at the two of them.

"What position is that?" Raelyn ask shifting in her seat.

"And the bitch dumb." Tan mumbled loud enough for everyone to hear.

"You will soon find out." He responded and looked over at the butler.

"Can you please ask my friends in the office to join us?" he instructed.

"Right away Senor." The butler stated and disappeared from the room.

He squeezed my shoulders and said, "Senorita Jazzel, do you mind moving to the head of the table."

"Of course," She responded as he pulled her chair out for her.

"John and Tangela can you move down as well?" he instructed.

They did as they were instructed as Angelo resumed his announcement,

"As I was saying." Angelo said looking around the table. "There are going to be some changes in the organization."

"What kind of changes?" Santiago asked just as the door to the dining room swung open. Tiffany entered the room looking like she just stepped off the runway.

"Hola Senorita." Angelo said embracing her. "Where's my friend?' he asked looking behind her.

"Senor Knight had to stop at the restroom." The butler stated.

"Jazzell ... Tan... both you ladies know my good friend Tiffany." Angelo said, Tan and I both smiled and nodded.

"Tiffany this is Senor John, Santiago, and his good friend Raelyn." He continued going around the table.

Then the door opened again and in walked Ace, smiling.

"And this is my good friend Ace. But he needs no introduction. I think we all know him." Angelo laughed putting his arm around Ace. Ace smile quickly disappeared as he looked around the table and locked eyes on Jazzy.

Jazzy was stuck, she couldn't move, she couldn't talk, her heart was beating so fast, she could feel it in her ears.

"What the fuck!" Tan said again, but this time she was loudly.

Big John remained quiet with a straight face. Raelyn sat there clueless and Santiago face wore a look of shock.

"Have a seat my friend." Angelo instructed, pointing to the chair at the opposite end of the table. He pulled out the chair directly beside him for Tiffany.

"Look around." Angelo stated. "Do you see how everyone is positioned at the table?"

No one said a word.

"This is the new set up for this organization. Ace and Jazzel at the head and everyone in between."

"Yo what the fuck are you talking bout Angelo? Nobody got time for your riddles and shit." Santiago huffed.

Angelo shot him an evil look and continued.

"Let me break it down so that we are all on the same page. We are taking over the city. Ace and Tiffany will run the South and West side and Jazzel and Tan will continue to run the East and North side." he announced. "All the corner boys and runners will report to the soldiers, such as yourself Santiago, and soldiers report to Tan or Tiffany. Tan and Tiffany report to Ace and Jazzel. And they report directly to me. One big happy drug dealing family!" Angelo explained, laughing.

"Wait, how yall just gonna take over my grandfathers' shit like that?" Raelyn asked.

"It's really quite easy my dear." Angelo answered walking over to the phone in the corner. He picked it up and spoke softly and quickly into the phone with his back turned to us.

"This is some bullshit Angelo. I have put in a lot of work for you, and you keep shitting on me." Santiago yelled.

Angelo hung up the phone and turned to face him.

"I knew you would feel that way Santiago. Even though I was hoping you wouldn't." he admitted.

"I can't just sit back and let this shit go down." Raelyn yelled scooting her chair back.

"There's nothing you can do to stop it. Too bad you're not going to be around to see it unfold." Angelo stated just as 4 big ass security guards entered the room.

"Take them to the basement. I will deal with them later." He commanded and the security guards grabbed both Raelyn and Santiago and snatched them out of their chairs. They moved so quick, Santiago didn't have time to pull his gun.

The butler grabbed the gun out of Santiago's waist as they were being dragged out of the room kicking and screaming.

The room was quiet for a moment as everyone was in disbelief about the turn of events.

"So, this is the Queen who've been telling me so much about." Ace said breaking the silence. His gaze never leaving Jazzy.

"And you are his Ace in the Hole." Jazzy responded, she felt as if she wanted to cry and curse, but she held her composure.

"Now that everyone is acquainted let's move this party to the lanai, it's such a beautiful evening we should enjoy it." Angelo sang.

Everyone got up from their seats and were escorted to the lanai, where Angelo had spread fit for royalty set up.

Ace walked over to Jazzy.

"It's good to see you. You look amazing. I see you been doing yo thang while I been gone." He admired.

Jazzy looked at him with tears in her eyes.

"Where you been? What's up with this shit? Is this how you come back into my life?" she cried.

"No Jazzy it's not like that." he pleaded.

"Cut the shit Ace. I know you." she yelled. "What you failed to realize is I'm not the same Jazzy you left months ago, a lot has changed."

"I see." Ace said sarcastically, looking her up and down.

"You think you gonna pop back up and I let you take over my shit? My Papa's streets? Just because I loved you at one point? You out yo rabbit ass mind!" She said through clinched teeth.

"I aint trying to take over shit.... And what you me loved me at one point? You don't love me no more?" he tested.

"Nigga that love faded just like you did when you left without a word." Jazzy threw back.

"Oh wow." Ace exclaimed. "So, I guess we beefing now? No more Bonnie and Clyde?" he asked jokingly trying to lighten the tension.

Jazzy chuckled and said "I learned a long time ago, playing Bonnie will have you fucked up out here and Clyde gonna be gone."

"Jazzy" Ace pleaded.

"My name is Jazzel." She corrected.

He stepped back and looked at her like she was crazy.

"Look" she continued. "I'm gonna go along with this plan. But it won't be for long. I hate sharing. But you know this already."

"Yeah, and you that I didn't give a damn who you are or were to me, I don't take threats kindly." He stated walking closer.

"Yes, I know this. But there is another thing that we both know baby." She said softening her voice, as she ran her fingers along the trim of his suit jacket.

"Oh, Yeah What's that?" Ace responded licking his lips.

"There can only be one ruler in the kingdom. Never try to play the Queen she is the she most important piece on the board." Jazzel responded.

He smirked "If you gonna sit at the table with the big dogs you must learn the most important rule of the game.

"Which is?" she tested.

He looked her deep in her eyes and whispered, "In this game the Ace of Spades always trumps the Queen."

42401034R00120

Made in the USA
Middletown, DE
10 April 2017